Nedko Solakov

Nedko Solakov

Romantic Landscapes with Missing Parts

Neuer Berliner Kunstverein
4. Mai bis 16. Juni 2002

Ulmer Museum
7. Juli bis 1. September 2002

Hatje Cantz

Erschienen anlässlich der Ausstellung/
Published on the occasion of the exhibition

Nedko Solakov
Romantic Landscapes with Missing Parts

Herausgeber/Editor
Neuer Berliner Kunstverein, Alexander Tolnay
Ulmer Museum, Brigitte Reinhardt

Übersetzungen/Translations
Lucinda Rennison
(Deutsch – Englisch)

Katalogkonzept und Gestaltung
Nedko Solakov
Ralf Henning

Reproduktion/Reproduction
Elch-Graphics, Berlin

Gesamtherstellung/Printed by
Dr. Cantz'sche Druckerei, Ostfildern-Ruit

© 2002 Hatje Cantz Verlag, Ostfildern-Ruit,
und Autoren/and authors
© 2002 für die abgebildeten Werke von
Solakov bei dem Künstler
© 2002 for the reproduced works of
Solakov by the artist

Erschienen bei/Published by
Hatje Cantz Publishers
Senefelderstraße 12
73760 Ostfildern-Ruit
Deutschland/Germany
Tel. + 49/711/4 40 50
Fax + 49/711/4 40 52 20
Internet: www.hatjecantz.de

Distribution in the US
D.A.P., Distributed Art Publishers, Inc.
155 Avenue of the Americas, Second Floor
New York, N.Y. 10013-1507
USA
Tel. + 1/212/6 27 19 99
Fax + 1/212/6 27 94 84

ISBN 3-7757-9117-5

Printed in Germany

Umschlagabbildung
Nedko Solakov

Fotos/Photos
Andrea Stappert
Angel Tzvetanov
Anna Kleberg
Arpad Farkas
Blaise Adilon
Eileen Costa
Gianni Romano
Giorgio Colombo
Johann Koinegg
Josif Kiraly
Kees Moeliker
Lazslo Jaksity
Mads Gamdrop
Mariusz Michalski
Anatoli Michailov
Nedko Solakov
Pierre Leguillon
Roberto Marossi
Shestakov
Tom Powel Imaging, Inc.
Ursula Seitz-Gray

Gedruckt mit finanzieller Unterstützung
der Deutschen Klassenlotterie Berlin unter
Befürwortung der Senatsverwaltung für
Wissenschaft, Forschung und Kultur, Berlin

Printed with the financial support of the
Deutsche Klassenlotterie Berlin, under the
auspieces of the Berlin Senat's Department
for Science, Research and Culture

Vorwort
Foreword

Nedko Solakov ist zweifelsohne der international bekannteste und in seiner Heimat angesehenste Künstler der jüngeren Generation Bulgariens. Wie sein berühmter Landsmann Christo, der im Gegensatz zu ihm Bulgarien früh verlassen hat, erhielt Solakov eine handwerklich perfekte Ausbildung an der Kunstakademie in Sofia. Er erwarb dort ein ähnlich meisterhaftes malerisches und zeichnerisches Können, das er trotz seiner künstlerischen Entwicklung in eine konzeptuelle Richtung stets als wirkungsvolles Mittel beibehielt. Auch in seinem neuesten Werk „Romantic Landscapes with Missing Parts", das in Berlin und in Ulm zum ersten Mal präsentiert wird, bedient er sich des traditionellen Mediums Malerei und verlängert es mit dem ihm eigenen Humor in eine geistreich-ironische Rauminstallation.

Die Themen von Solakovs Arbeiten der letzten zehn Jahre, die wir in dieser Publikation ebenfalls vorstellen, kreisen um die Zwiespältigkeiten des Alltags, der Sprache, des Verhaltens von Menschen und des Kunstbetriebs. Die Auswahl reicht von der symbolgeladenen „Neue Arche Noah" aus dem Jahr 1992 bis zu der interaktiven Installation „A Life (Black & White)", mit der der Bulgare bei der Biennale Venedig 2001 große Anerkennung errang. Die Werke kreisen stets um einen zentralen Punkt, das Absurde, wie es in der allgegenwärtigen Kluft zwischen Ideal und Wirklichkeit aufscheint.

Wir danken Nedko Solakov für die anregende und freundschaftliche Zusammenarbeit, für die Einrichtung der „Romantic Landscapes with Missing Parts" in den sehr unterschiedlichen Räumen in Berlin und in Ulm sowie für die Konzeption des Katalogbuches, die er zusammen mit dem Graphiker Ralf Henning, dem ebenfalls unser Dank gilt, kreativ und sorgfältig ausgearbeitet hat.

Alexander Tolnay
Neuer Berliner Kunstverein

Among Bulgarian artists of the younger generation, Nedko Solakov is the best-known internationally and the most respected in his home country. Like his famous compatriot Christo, who – by contrast – left Bulgaria early on in his life, Solakov received training in perfect technique and craftsmanship at the Academy of Fine Arts in Sofia. There he acquired a similar mastery of painting and drawing, which he has always retained as an effective means despite his artistic development in a conceptual direction. In his latest work, "Romantic Landscapes with Missing Parts", which is being presented for the first time in Berlin and Ulm, he also makes use of the traditional medium of painting, expanding upon it with his own particular sense of humour to create an ingenious, ironical spatial installation.

Solakov's works dating from the last ten years, which we are also presenting in this publication, revolve around the conflicts of everyday life, of language, of people's behaviour and of the art business. The selection ranges from the symbolically loaded "New Noah's Ark" from the year 1992 to the interactive installation "A Life (Black & White)", which brought the Bulgarian great acclaim at the Venice Biennial in 2001. The variety of expressive forms and the richness of content in his work is astonishing. His oeuvre has always revolved around a central point, the absurd – demonstrating the way in which this reveals itself in the omnipresent rift between the ideal and reality.

We are grateful to Nedko Solakov for his stimulating and friendly collaboration, for setting up the "Romantic Landscapes with Missing Parts" in very different rooms in Berlin and Ulm, and for his conception of the catalogue book, which has been thoroughly and creatively realised together with the graphic designer Ralf Henning, whom we should also like to thank at this point.

Brigitte Reinhardt
Ulmer Museum

Inhalt / Contents

5

Das ständig wieder begonnene Spiel der Vorstellungskraft

Zu den „Romantic Landscapes with Missing Parts" von Nedko Solakov

The Constantly Resumed Game of Imagination

On the „Romantic Landscapes with Missing Parts" by Nedko Solakov

Nedko Solakov rechnet mit Betrachtern („the average global citizen"[1]), denen Elemente der deutschen Romantik entweder als Klischee oder als nostalgisches Lebensgefühl gegenwärtig sind. Diese Doppelperspektive ist triftig. Denn manche Betrachter schwanken zwischen unmittelbarer Wahrnehmung und intellektueller Wertschätzung hin und her. Deshalb hat Solakov die beiden Serien „Romantischer Landschaften mit fehlenden Teilen" (2000/02) so angelegt, daß sie sowohl Ironiker als auch Naive interessieren können. Denn nur mit einer Doppelperspektive kann er gegenüber einem als gespalten angenommenen Publikum auch die für das Romantische wesentliche Kategorie der Interaktion[2] instrumentieren und zugleich durch ironische Ambivalenz brechen. Deshalb handelt es sich nicht um eine Revitalisierung von Stereotypen der deutschen Romantik, sondern um eine zweischneidige Humoreske, die sich mild selbst parodiert. Ich werde im Folgenden zeigen, daß Nedko Solakov mit den Konstruktionsprinzipien Caspar David Friedrichs (1774-1840) ein Versteckspiel veranstaltet und versucht, die Ironiker mit den Naiven zu versöhnen.

Was läßt sich als Klischee und als Lebensgefühl des Romantischen in der bildenden Kunst festhalten? „Nach Innen geht der geheimnisvolle Weg. In uns oder nirgends ist die Ewigkeit mit ihren Welten, die Vergangenheit und Zukunft."[3] Diesen von Novalis vorgeschlagenen Königsweg in romantische Abgründe schlug Solakov aus. Er näherte sich dem Romantischen über bereits vermittelte Werke, orientierte sich an Bildern im Museum und ihren Surrogaten in einfachen Hotelzimmern und setzt ihre wiederkehrenden Elemente zu einer Phantasie über das Romantische als Pop-Romantik zusammen. Das Romantische gilt Solakov als Ausstellungsprojekt. Es ist ein selbstgesetzter Plan, den er erfüllt. Eine Anschauung der Welt, die er elementar teilen und für die heutige Zeit aktualisieren würde, verbindet er selbst damit nicht. Ihn interessiert die populäre Wirkungsgeschichte der Romantik, nicht die Ideen der Romantiker. Er will eine Ausstellung inszenieren, keine romantische Idee. Deshalb zitie-

Nedko Solakov reckons with viewers ("the average global citizen"[1]) who are familiar with elements of the German romantic period, either as clichés or as a nostalgic vital awareness. This double perspective is convincing, for many viewers waver continually between direct perception and intellectual appreciation. This is why Solakov structured the two series of "Romantic Landscapes with Missing Parts" (2000/2002) so that they might interest both the ironic and the naïve viewer. Only with a double perspective is it possible for him – in face of a divided public – to instrumentalise the category of interaction[2] so essential to Romanticism, and at the same time to break through it with an ironical ambivalence. For this reason, we are not dealing with a revitalisation of stereotypes from German Romanticism, but with a two-edged humoresque, mildly parodying itself. In the following, I shall demonstrate the fact that Nedko Solakov creates a game of hide-and-seek using the constructive principles of Caspar David Friedrich (1774-1840), thus seeking to reconcile the ironic with the naïve.

What may be grasped as cliché and what as vital awareness of the romantic in fine art? "The mysterious path leads inwards. Eternity with its worlds, the past and the future, is within us or nowhere at all."[3] Solakov rejected this royal route to romantic depths suggested by Novalis. He approached the romatic via works already readily available, orienting himself on pictures in museums and their surrogates in simple hotel rooms, and assembling their recurrent elements into a fantasy about the romantic as Pop-Romanticism. The romantic, for Solakov, is to be regarded as an exhibition project. It is a self-imposed plan he is fulfilling. He himself sees no connection with a view of the world he would divide up in an elementary way, bringing it up-to-date for this day and age. He is interested in the popular history of Romanticism's influence, and not in the ideas of the Romanticists. He wants to stage an exhibition, not a romantic idea. For that reason, his oil paintings cite the pictorial rhetoric of German Romanticism, but at the same time they deny that they are romantic pictures.

Giving and taking at the same time, arriving and simultaneously bidding farewell, proximity and a simultaneous distance;

... the lovers' bench.

... the castle.

... all the profound thoughts in the philosopher's head.

Studies for Romantic Landscapes with Missing Parts (and tips for the average global citizen)
2000; Öl auf Leinwandkarton, eine Serie von 12 Stück; je 25,4 x 35,6 cm/ oil on canvas board, a series of 12 pieces; 25,4 x 35,6 cm each.
Courtesy Galerie Arndt & Partner und/and der Künstler/the artist.

ren die Oberflächen seiner Ölbilder die Bildrhetorik der deutschen Romantik, dementieren aber sogleich, daß es sich um romantische Bilder handelt.

Geben bei gleichzeitigem Nehmen, Ankunft bei gleichzeitigem Abschied, Nähe bei gleichzeitiger Ferne, dieser performative Widerspruch strukturiert als ironische Grundfigur neben vorherigen Arbeiten „Romantic Landscapes with Missing Parts". Der Neue Berliner Kunstverein und anschließend das Ulmer Museum zeigen zwölf goldgerahmte Ölgemälde. Sie beziehen sich auf die parallel gezeigten Ölstudien in der Berliner Galerie Arndt & Partner, sind aber in den Motiven nicht allesamt identisch. Ausser dem Anschein des Romantischen verbindet alle 24 Bilder das Motiv des Verlusts. Mal fehlt der Mond, mal ein Boot, mal ein Vogelschwarm, mal eine Lichtspiegelung.

Seiner Idee, romantische Landschaften mit Fehlstellen zu malen, und die Studien und Gemälde parallel zu zeigen, um das Ganze gewitzt als Auseinandersetzung zu präsentieren, folgte die handwerkliche Ausführung. Sie schloß für den Konzeptkünstler ein, sich an das Ein-Mal-Eins der Ölmalerei aus seiner Zeit an der Kunstakademie in Sofia zu erinnern (siehe Solakovs Statement in diesem Katalog). Überdies hatte er sich mit Kompositionsprinzipien vertraut zu machen. Er entschied sich für Landschaftsmalerei, dem Inbegriff des Romantischen, wie er sich durch Caspar David Friedrich, John Constable, den frühen JMW Turner im Norden Europas lind und lieblich bilden und für populäre Lesarten prägen konnte. Die Romantik Frankreichs – etwa von Eugène Delacroix – spielt in der ironisch ambivalenten Version Solakovs ebensowenig eine Rolle wie der Orientalismus englischer und französischer Romantiker oder gar die fiebrig-verwegenen Satiren und gewaltgesättigten Landschaften Francisco Goyas. Solakov widmet sich der Romantik nicht im Sinne einer Revision, vielmehr der Vorstellung einer idealen Harmonie in den Bildern eines kleinen, aber wirkungsvollen Teils romantischer Maler. Und auch bei diesen – etwa Friedrich – übergeht er ebenso die kaltgemalten Verkantungen wie sie in „Die gescheiterte Hoffnung" offenbar werden wie architekturbestimmte Ansichten oder panoramatische Stadtlandschaften. Solakov will die heimelige Hausversion des Romantischen.

Er bevorzugt den weichen Schwung im Dämmerlicht. Es ist immer Abend oder Morgengrauen. Die Nacht regiert die Farben und macht sie stumpf und sänftigend. Menschen, falls sie überhaupt vorkommen, sind klein wie Ameisen in weiter Ferne verloren. Doch gekrümmte Perspektiven, Kontrast zwischen Nähe und Ferne, Axialsymmetrie verdanken viel den Konstruktionsprinzipien von Caspar David Friedrich. Auch Solakov teilt den Raum

as a basic ironic figure, this performative contradiction not only structures previous works, but also "Romantic Landscapes with Missing Parts." The Neuer Berliner Kunstverein is showing twelve oil paintings in golden frames. They are related to oil studies being shown parallel to them in the Berlin gallery Arndt & Partner, but their motifs are not all identical. Apart from the impression of the romantic, all 24 pictures are linked by the motif of loss. Sometimes the moon is missing, sometimes a boat, a flock of birds, or a reflection of light.

The artist's idea to paint romantic landscapes with missing parts – and to exhibit the studies and the paintings parallel to each other in order to cleverly present the whole as discursive – was followed by its technical realisation. For the conceptual artist, this involved a recollection of the basics of oil painting learnt during his time at the Academy of Art in Sofia (see Solakov's statement in this catalogue). In addition, he had to become familiar with principles of composition. He decided in favour of a form of landscape painting seen as the epitome of romanticism; the landscape which was able to evolve, mild and charming, in the work of Caspar David Friedrich, John Constable and the early JMW Turner in the north of Europe, ideally suited to popular interpretations. The Romanticism of France – for example by Eugène Delacroix – plays as little part in Solakov's ironic, ambivalent version as the orientalism of English and French Romanticists or the feverishly bold satires and landscapes awash with violence painted by Francisco Goya. Solakov does not devote himself to Romanticism in the sense of a revision, but far more to the notion of ideal harmony found in the pictures of a small but influential number of romantic painters. And even in the case of these – Friedrich, for example – he passes over coldly painted cants like those revealed in "Die gescheiterte Hoffnung" (Disappointed Hope) as well as architecturally defined views or panoramic cityscapes. Solakov wants the cosy, domestic version of the romantic.

He has a preference for gentle slopes in twilight. It is always evening or dawn. The night governs the colours, making them dull and calming. People, if they appear at all, are as tiny as ants, lost in the far distance. But these curving perspectives, the contrast between proximity and distance, the axial symmetry owe much to Caspar David Friedrich's principles of construction. Solakov also divides the space into a limited foreground we may enter in our imagination, and an infinite background which it is impossible to pass into. This world and the world beyond are set in opposition, and it is possible to grasp this pictorially. This construction demands that our perception develop a different way of seeing and of understanding images: that is, creating an imaginary link between a vague, transported distance and a solid foreground, although the image lacks a bridging, central sphere. A view to the horizon is only possible across a chasm. Solakov has made this into the principle of both series. The things which one does not

oft in einen begrenzten, imaginär betretbaren Vordergrund und einen unendlichen Hintergrund, der in der Vorstellung nicht zu betreten ist. Das Diesseits und das Jenseits werden in eine piktoral fassliche Opposition gesetzt. Die Konstruktion fordert von der Wahrnehmung eine andere Art des Sehens und Bildverstehens, nämlich die Trennung zwischen vag entrückter Ferne und stabil präsenter Nähe ohne einen überbrückenden Mittelgrund in der Vorstellung zu verbinden. Der Blick, der den Horizont berührt, ist nur über einen Abgrund möglich. Dies hat Solakov zum Prinzip beider Serien gemacht. Das, was man nicht sieht, von dessen Existenz man aber weiß oder zu wissen glaubt, spielt in romantischen Bildern eine vielfach variierte Rolle, bei Friedrich ist es das Wesentliche.[4]

Solakov übernimmt die Technik, nicht den Glauben an die Durchdringung von Innen und Aussen, Dieseitigem und Jenseitigem. Friedrich schrieb: „Der Mensch soll nicht malen, was er vor sich sieht, sondern was er in sich sieht. Sieht er aber nichts in sich, so unterlasse er auch zu malen, was er vor sich sieht."[5] Solakov hat dieser Innenschau allesüberspringend mit seiner Doppelschau geantwortet.

Friedrich konstruierte seine Landschaften so genau wie ein Architekt einen Bauplan. Auf Anregung seines Freundes Carl Gustav Carus (1789-1869) und dessen „Neun Briefen über Landschaftsmalerei" (1831) erarbeitete er einen Katalog von Standardisierungen und skizzierte vor Ort, was sich als Ansichten von Tälern, Mulden, Bäumen, Felsen, Bergen, Seen zeichenhaft verwenden und standardisieren ließ. Im Atelier setzte er die Zeichen je nach Bedarf als Chiffren für Stimmungen gezielt in die Gesamtkomposition ein. Die atmosphärische Gestimmtheit, die tief empfunden und wie aus einem Guss ermalt erscheint, war Ergebnis einer wohlüberlegten Konstruktion aus Standardisierungen vielfach weit auseinanderliegender Einzelteile. Diesem Prinzip folgte Solakov und macht witzige Bilderrätsel daraus, in dem er Chiffren weglässt und das Weggelassene im Bildtitel benennt. Unter dem Blick von Friedrich wird die Naturanschauung eine konfigurierte Landschaft – ein Gegenstand bewußt bildbezogener Betrachtung als artifizielles Phantasma. Es hört wohl deshalb nicht auf, Ironiker und Naive zu interessieren, weil es Friedrich gelingt, zwischen der Natur als Zeichen und den Zeichen der Natur die Balance zu halten und beide Lesarten in Fülle belohnt. Unter dem Blick von Solakov wird sowohl die bildbezogene Betrachtung parodiert, als auch mit der Konfiguration aus Standards ein Versteckspiel der Chiffren veranstaltet. Der Reiz liegt im Fort-Da-Spiel (dessen psychoanalytisch-orientierte Lektüre wir hier ebenso übergehen wie das Motiv des Doppelgängers).

see, but of whose existence one is aware, or believes in, play a diverse and varied role in romantic paintings; in the case of Friedrich, this is the essential aspect.[4]

Solakov adopts the technique, not the belief in a permeation of inside and outside, of this world and the next. Friedrich wrote: "A person should not paint what he sees before him, but what he sees within himself. If he sees nothing within himself, he should also refrain from painting what he sees before him."[5] Leaving everything out, Solakov has responded to this interior vista with his own double presentation.

Friedrich constructed his landscapes with as much precision as an architect conceiving his building plan. Stimulated by his friend Carl Gustav Carus (1789-1869) and the latter's "Nine Letters on Landscape Painting" (1831), he worked out a catalogue of standard features, sketching whatever could be standardised and used in a symbolic way on the spot; views of valleys, hollows, trees, rocks, mountains or lakes. Back in his studio, he set the symbols as ciphers revealing mood or atmosphere into the overall composition as he required them. The atmospheric mood, which appears to be deeply-felt and painted as a unified whole, was the result of a well thought out construction based on standard features; individual parts often widely distributed. Solakov also followed this principle, making it into witty picture riddles by leaving out ciphers, naming whatever he had left out in the picture title. In the eyes of Friedrich, contemplation of nature becomes a configured landscape – an object of consciously picture – related contemplation as an artificial phantasm. This is probably the reason why those who are ironic and those who are naïve both continue to find his work so interesting, as Friedrich succeeds in keeping a balance between nature as a symbol and the symbols of nature, so rewarding both ways of interpreting his work fully. Seen through Solakov's eyes, the picture-related contemplation is parodied, and a game of hide-and-seek with ciphers is also played using the configuration from standard features. The attraction lies in the game of "now you see it, now you don't" (the psychoanalytically oriented reading of which we shall pass over here, along with the motif of the double).

In autumn 2001, Solakov limited himself to a bright, wide and empty room in his exhibition "Chat" in the IASPIS in Stockholm, exhibiting no objects, but permitting the room itself to speak. In the smallest possible writing, he drew speech bubbles referring to architectural elements on the walls. A small hole gaped just above the skirting board. Beside this he drew an arrow and noted: "a major hole (one of the BIGGEST in this VERY room)." Above the door frame he painted a little man and wrote beside him: "I am stupid and I kind of like it". On the wall he wrote: "Why do I have to follow the stupid curves of this old fashioned greyish stuff? Where are my white

... the sailor's boat.

... some segments of a certain sunbeam.

... the fire.

Im Herbst 2001 hatte sich Solakov in seiner Ausstellung „Chat" im IASPIS in Stockholm auf einen hellen weiten, leeren Raum beschränkt, in dem er keine Objekte ausstellte, sondern den Raum selbst sprechen ließ. Er schrieb an die Wände in kleiner Handschrift Sprechblasen zu Architekturelementen. Knapp über der Fußleiste klaffte ein kleines Loch. Daneben zeichnete er einen Pfeil und notierte: „a major hole (one of the BIGGEST in this VERY room)". Über den Türrahmen malte er ein Männchen und schrieb daneben: „I am stupid and I kind of like it". An die Wand schrieb er: „Why do I have to follow the stupid curves of this old fashioned greyish stuff? Where are my white cube's corners?" Der Raum mit seinen Gegebenheiten machte vielstimmig auf seine Beschaffenheit und zahlreiche Kunstreferenze aufmerksam. Er konnte als Parodie zu Yves Kleins epochemachender Einladung in einen leeren weißen Galerienraum von Iris Clert am 28. April 1958, um 21 Uhr, verstanden werden. „Das, was wir Leere nennen", so Klein anläßlich dieser 'Ausstellung des Immateriellen', „ist nicht das, was das Sein umschließt, noch das, was seine Löcher ausfüllt: es ist die Energie eines ständig wieder begonnen Spiels."[6] Solakovs Inszenierung des Raums gewann seine Eigentümlichkeit durch seine Insistenz auf kleine und kleinste Details. Der weiße Raum war nicht leer. Das Kleinste und Beiläufigeste gewann eine komödiantisch-spöttische Stimme und Resonanz im Reflexionswinkel der Kunstgeschichte seit der zweiten Hälfte des 20. Jahrhunderts und dessen Sackgasse, in die sie Klein hineinmanöveriert zu haben glaubte. Die Schau partizipierte an der Kraft die vom Verspotteten und Parodierten ausging.

Der performative Widerspruch durch werkinterne Oppositionen hat Strukturähnlichkeiten zu Sprach- und Denkformen wie sie das Barock und der Manierismus kultivierte. François Villon „stirbt vor Durst an der Quelle". Solche Sprach- und Denkweisen erscheinen durch dekonstruktivistische Verfahren der letzten Jahrzehnte, an denen auch Solakov teilhat, in neuem Licht. „Unentscheidbarkeit" und „performativer Widerspruch" sind mächtige Kategorien gegen die „Widerspruchsfreiheit" positivistischer Diskurse geworden. Solakov wehrt sich mit Ausstellungen narrativer Tendenz gegen alles, was widerspruchsfrei zu sein hat. Oft inkorporieren sie eine Zeitdimension. Immer aber spielt Sprache und ihre Kraft, Vorstellungen zu erzeugen, in eine andere Welt zu entführen oder einen Witz explodieren zu lassen, eine wesentliche Rolle. Die Kritikerin Kim Levin hat nach einer Reflexion über Solakovs Herkunft aus einem ehemaligen Satellitenstaat der UDSSR darauf hingewiesen, sein Werk „resonates with the liberating energies and confusions of colliding systems. His careering narratives

cube's corners?" In many ways, the room and its conditions drew attention to its overall state and made numerous references to art. It could be understood as a parody of Yves Klein's epoch-making invitation to an empty, white room in Iris Clert's gallery on April 28th 1958 at 9pm. "What we call emptiness", as Klein said on the occasion of this 'exhibition of the immaterial', "is not what encompasses being, nor is it that which fills its spaces: it is the energy of a constantly resumed game"[6]. Solakov's staged presentation of the room gained its character by means of an insistence on small, even the smallest details. The white room was not empty. The smallest and most casual detail developed a theatrical, mocking voice and resonance with its reflection of art history since the second half of the 20th century, and of the dead end into which Klein believed he had manoeuvred art. The exhibition participated in the force emanating from things mocked and parodied.

This performative contradiction arising from oppositions within the work has structural similarities to forms of speech and thought cultivated by Mannerism and the Baroque. Francois Villon "died of thirst at the spring". Such manners of speaking and thinking appear in a new light as a result of the deconstructivist processes during recent decades, in which Solakov has also participated. "The impossibility of decision" and "performative contradiction" have become powerful categories opposing the "freedom from contradiction" of positivist discourse. Solakov defends himself against everything which has to be free of contradiction with exhibitions of a narrative tendency. Often they incorporate the dimension of time. But language and its power always play a decisive role in creating ideas, abducting us into another world or exploding a gag. The critic Kim Levin — after reflecting on Solakov's origins from a former satellite state of the USSR — pointed out that his work "resonates with the liberating energies and confusions of colliding systems. His careering narratives exult in exhilarating freedom. (…) Solakov's absurd narratives and installations evoke a deconstructed world that has lost its faith and ideals."[7] He sets absurdity against meaning, deviation against linear progression, and his constantly resumed game against end-games and the ideology of dead ends. It is a game beginning with the sentence he has employed as a leitmotiv in several staged presentations: "Just imagine..." This sentence is also a leitmotiv running through everything which may be called "romantic", reconciling the ironic viewer with the naïve.

... the moon itself.

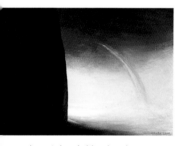

... the rainbow's blue band.

... the mountain's reflection on the tranquil surface of the lake.

exult in exhilerating freedom. (..) Solakov's absurd narratives and installations evoke a deconstructed world that has lost its faith and ideals."[7] Gegen Sinn setzt er Absurdität, gegen lineare Progression Abweichung, gegen die Endspiele und die Ideologie der Sackgassen sein ständig wieder begonnenes Spiel, das mit dem Satz beginnt, den er in mehreren Inszenierungen als Leitmotiv verwandte: „Stellen Sie sich vor..." Dieser Satz zieht sich auch leitmotivisch durch alles, was „romantisch" genannt werden darf und versöhnt die Ironiker mit den Naiven.

Peter Herbstreuth

Anmerkungen:

1 Der Arbeitstitel, an dem Nedko Solakov bis in die Ausstellungsvorbereitungen festhielt, lautete: „Romantic Landscapes with missing parts (and tips for the average global citizen)."

2 Ein romantische Werk belehrt den Betrachter, Leser, Hörer nicht. Es spricht zu ihm als Gleichem, fordert zum Dialog und durch Anspielungen, Lücken, Sprünge zur Teilnahme. Daher auch die Kultivierung des Fragments – als Anregung der Imagination zur Interaktion. „Der wahre Leser muß der erweiterte Autor sein", schrieb Novalis (Frhr. von Hardenberg), zit. nach Anna-Maria Ehrmann-Schindlbeck: Imagination Romantik; in: Imagination Romantik, Kulturamt der Stadt Jena (Hg), Jena 2001; S. 20

3 Novalis (Frhr. von Hardenberg): Schriften, Bd. II. H.-J. Müller/R. Samuel (Hg), Darmstadt 1999; S. 232.

4 vgl. Helmut Börsch-Supan: Die ersten Dresdner Jahre Caspar David Friedrichs. In: Dresdner Hefte 58. Beiträge zur Kulturgeschichte. Dresden und die Anfänge der Romantik: Dresdner Geschichtsverein (Hg), Dresden 1999; S. 71

5 siehe Anm. 2; S. 20

6 siehe: Michel Guèrin: La Terreur et la Pietié, 1 – La Terreur, Arles, 1990; S. 3105.

7 Kim Levin: Nedko Solakov-Marginalia; In: Nedko Solakov: Stories 1/Historie 1, Center for Contemporary Art Ujazdowski Castle, Warsaw (Hg), Warsaw 2000

Notes:

1 The draft title on which Nedko Solakov kept hold to until the exhibition preparations was: "Romantic Landscapes with Missing Parts (and tips for the average global citizen)"

2 A romantic work does not seek to educate the viewer, reader or audience. It speaks to him as an equal, calling for dialogue and participation by means of allusion, gaps, or leaps in thought. This is the reason for cultivating the fragment – as a stimulus of the imagination to interaction. "The true reader must be an extension of the author", Novalis (Freiherr von Hardenberg) wrote, cited from Anna-Maria Ehrmann-Schindlbeck: Imagination Romantik; in: Imagination Romantik, Kulturamt der Stadt Jena (ed.), Jena 2001; p. 20

3 Novalis (Freiherr von Hardenberg): Schriften, Vol. II, H.-J. Müller/R. Samuel (eds.), Darmstadt 1999; p. 232

4 Compare Helmut Börsch-Supan; Die ersten Dresdner Jahre Caspar David Friedrichs. In: Dresdner Hefte 58. Beiträge zur Kulturgeschichte. Dresden und die Anfänge der Romantik: Dresdner Geschichtsverein (ed.), Dresden 1999; p. 71

5 See note 2; p. 20

6 See: Michel Guèrin: La Terreur et la Pietié, 1 – La Terreur, Arles, 1990; p. 3105

7 Kim Levin: Nedko Solakov – Marginalia; In: Nedko Solakov: Stories 1/Historie 1, Center for Contemporary Art Ujazdowski Castle, Warsaw (ed.), Warsaw 2000

... the flock of anxious birds.

... the exhausted pilgrim's tracks over the deep snow.

... the light in general.

... the moon itself

Romantic Landscapes with Missing Parts
2002; Öl auf Leinen, eine Serie von 12 Bildern, je 108 x 140 cm/
Oil on linen, a series of 12 paintings, 108 x 140 cm each
Courtesy der Künstler/*the artist*

The "Romantic Landscapes with Missing Parts" were executed in the murky winter of 2001/2 up north in Stockholm, in a nice studio situated in the Royal Academy of Fine Arts.

That was a very hard, horrible time for me – the conceptual artist, who pretends that I have a kind of advantage in being classically (mural painting) educated twenty years ago. Most of the time during these 3 months I was really pissed off by my inability to painterly achieve what I wanted (not to mention the bitter feeling that I was not quite sure what I did want actually). In such moments I had that enormous desire to close my eyes and all these canvases, oil paints, brushes, easel and palette to disappear and I to start dealing again with ideas (mainly) – a relatively easy (at least for me) way of working. But I kept doing the paintings, day by day, night after night, fiercely trying to accomplish them in an acceptable way for an audience like you.

"Why am I doing this?!" – I've been asking myself constantly, while one day I realised that perhaps the reason for me to keep going on was that I had that little hope that all missing from the romantic landscapes parts:

the moon itself;
the mountain's reflection on the tranquil surface of the lake;
the light in general;
the sailor's boat;
all the profound thoughts in the philosopher's head;
the flock of anxious birds;
the exhausted pilgrim's tracks over the deep snow;
Europa;
the castle on the top of the mountain;
the rainbow's violet band;
the purse of the wanderer (not the obviously unfinished painting);
the artist's concentration (a substantial part of the horizon goes unexpectedly down)…

…so, I had that little hope that all the missing parts will have a better and more interesting life when being outside the paintings.

Nedko Solakov
January, 2002
Stockholm

Die „Romantic Landscapes with Missing Parts" („Romantischen Landschaften mit fehlenden Teilen") wurden im düsteren Stockholmer Winter 2001/2 fertiggestellt, hoch im Norden in einem netten Studio der Königlichen Akademie der schönen Künste.

Das war eine sehr harte, eine schreckliche Zeit für mich – für den konzeptuellen Künstler, der sich vormachte, er hätte eine Art Vorteil, da er vor zwanzig Jahren klassisch ausgebildet wurde (Wandmalerei). Die meiste Zeit während dieser 3 Monate hatte ich die Faxen dicke, wegen meiner eigenen Unfähigkeit, malerisch das zu erreichen, was ich wollte, (geschweige denn das bittere Gefühl, dass ich mir das, was ich eigentlich wollte, nicht ganz sicher war). In solchen Momenten hatte ich den großen Wunsch, meine Augen zu schließen und alles – Leinwände, Öl-Farben, Pinsel, Staffelei und Palette – verschwinden zu lassen, damit ich mich wieder mit Ideen (hauptsächlich) beschäftigen könnte – eine (für mich jedenfalls) relativ einfache Art zu arbeiten. Aber ich schuf weiterhin die Gemälde, Tag für Tag, Nacht für Nacht, verbissen bemüht, sie für ein Publikum wie Sie akzeptabel zu machen.

„Warum tue ich das?!" habe ich mich ständig gefragt, aber eines Tages erkannte ich, dass eine kleine Hoffnung vielleicht der Grund war, weiterzumachen: Die Hoffnung, diese fehlenden Teile der romantischen Landschaften…

der Mond selbst;
die Spiegelung des Berges auf der ruhigen Oberfläche des Sees;
das Licht im allgemeinen;
das Boot des Seemannes;
alle tiefgründigen Gedanken im Kopf des Philosophen;
der Schwarm aufgeregter Vögel;
die Fährten des erschöpften Pilgers im tiefen Schnee;
Europa;
die Burg auf der Spitze des Berges;
das violette Band des Regenbogens;
das Portemonnaie des Wanderers (nicht das offensichtlich unfertige Gemälde)
die Konzentration des Künstlers (ein beträchtlicher Teil des Horizontes geht unerwartet unter)…

….also, ich hatte diese kleine Hoffnung, dass all die fehlenden Teile ein besseres und interesanteres Leben außerhalb der Gemälde haben würden.

handwritten on the wall

It is possible that the visitors instead of
looking at the beautiful winter landscape
with "the exhausted pilgrim's tracks over
the deep snow" missing, to discover
that there are tiny little stories
drawn/written directly on the walls
in a very subtle, discreet way, telling
the adventures of these tracks when
they are outside of the painting.
Stories like this one: the tracks
fall in love with lady's shoes (#43)...

… the exhausted pilgrim's tracks over the deep snow.

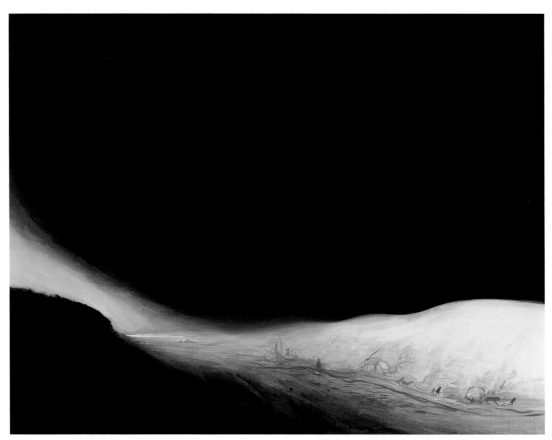

... the flock of anxious birds.

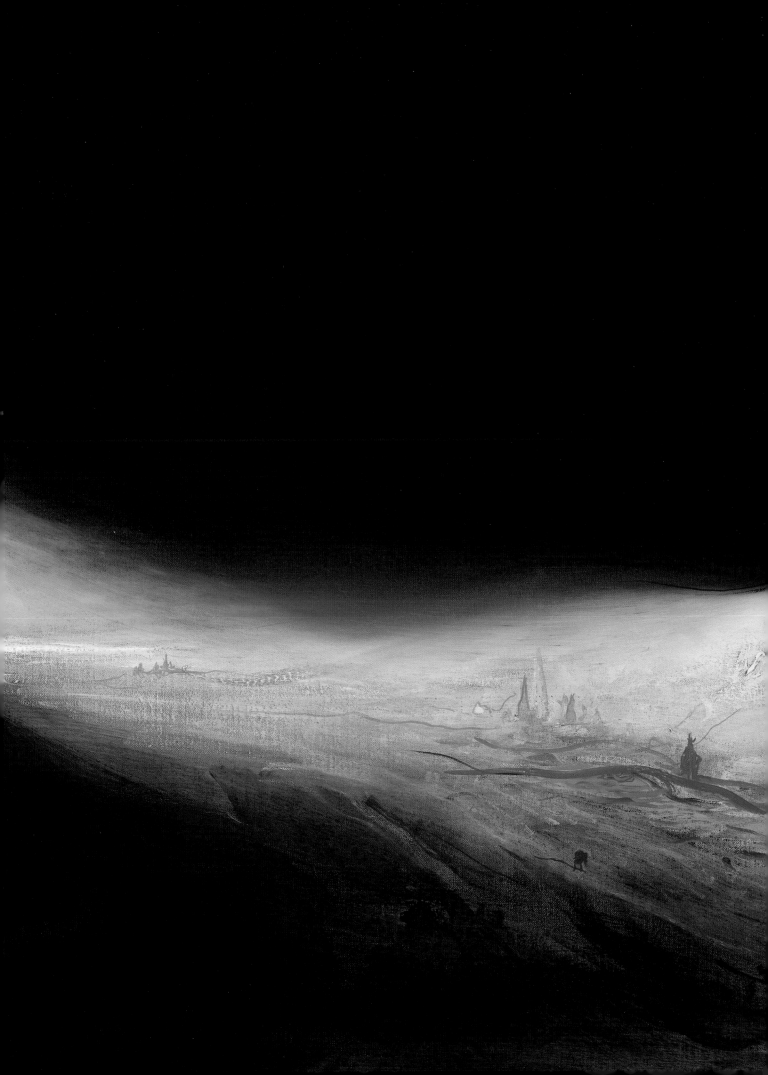

...the mountain's reflection on the tranquil surface of the lake.

...the purse of the wanderer (not the obviously unfinished painting).

... the light in general.

... all the profound thoughts in the philosopher's head.

...and then all the profound thoughts
from the philosopher's head said to themselves:
"But why we are still here – in this art institution?
Even if we are not in this kitschy painting,
out of that lazy bastard's head,
it is still not enough; we should
we must run away to the street,
even out of town!"
       – they were mumbling
             trying to get asleep
             in this cosy corner
                of the wall in front
                   of you....

... the rainbow's violet band.

... the artist's concentration (a substantial part of the horizon goes unexpectedly down).

the little boat was running
out of patience — the guy
or top of her was
so slow

… the sailor's boat.

… Europa.

... the castle on the top of the mountain.

FRÅNLUFTSFLÄKT
TEKNINGSSALEN

10   11   12

"why they
  hide
me   HERE?"
  - the remains of
      that (once much LARGER) yellow spot
           were talking to the switches board/box
              next to it. However
                the box kept a silence
                   (she didn't want to loose
                      her job by taking the side of that yellow loo...

a major hole
(one of the biggest
     in this VERY room)

Chat
2001; mixed-media, fast unsichtbar, auf den
Wänden der IASPIS Gallery, IASPIS, Stockholm /
*mixed, almost invisible, media on the walls of the
empty IASPIS Gallery, IASPIS, Stockholm.*
Courtesy der Künstler / *the artist* und / *and* IASPIS.

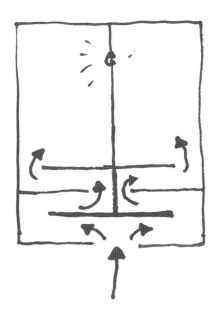

The Choice
2001; 2 Räume, blaue und gelbe Farbe, eine vergoldete, geschnitzte Truhe, blauer Samt, Füllmaterial,
Text, Stempel, eine Wächterin, die den Eingang
betreut / *2 rooms, blue and yellow paint, gilded carved
chest, blue velvet, filling material, text, stamp, guard
supervising entrance.* „Ein Raum ist eine Welt," Kunsthalle Zürich, 2001.
Courtesy der Künstler / *the artist* und / *and* Kunsthalle Zürich.

e)
...nd weiße Farbe; zwei Arbeiter/Maler, die die Wände des Ausstellungsraums kontinuierlich schwarz und weiß bemalen. Die Tätigkeit wird Tag ...dauer der Ausstellung ausgeführt (fünf Monate); variable Dimensionen/*black and white paint; two workers/painters constantly repainting the walls*

*of the exhibition space in black and white for the entire duration of the exhibition (five months), day after day (following each other); dimensions variable. „Plateau of Humankind,"
49. Biennale Venedig, 2001 / 49th Venice Biennale, 2001. Collection Susan and Lewis Manilow, Chicago; Sammlung Hauser und Wirth, St. Gallen. Courtesy der Künstler / the artist*

A Life (Black & White) 1998-2001

A Life (Black & White)
1998-2001; schwarze und weiße Farbe,
zwei Arbeiter/Maler, die die Wände des
Ausstellungsraums kontinuierlich schwarz
und weiß bemalen. Die Tätigkeit wird Tag
für Tag, für die Gesamtdauer der Ausstellung ausgeführt (fünf Monate)/*black
and white paint, two workers/painters constantly repainting the walls of the exhibition
space in black and white for the entire duration of the exhibition (five months), day after
day (following each other)*; variable Dimen-
sionen/*dimensions variable*; „Plateau of
Humankind," 49. Biennale Venedig, 2001/
49th Venice Biennale, 2001; Collection Susan
and Lewis Manilow, Chicago; Sammlung
Hauser und Wirth, St. Gallen.
Courtesy der Künstler/*the artist*.

Na ja, denke ich, als ich bei der Vorbesichtigung der
Biennale in Venedig 2001 durch einen Raum gehe, in dem
Wände gestrichen werden, die sind auch noch nicht fer-
tig. Dennoch bleibe ich vor dem Ausgang stehen, schaue
mich um. Ein Mann im Arbeitskittel weißelt, gegenüber
trägt ein anderer schwarze Wandfarbe auf, ruhig und
konzentriert in dem leeren Raum, dessen Mitte lediglich
ein paar Farbeimer und Malerwerkzeug besetzen. Schließ-
lich entdecke ich eine Beschriftung – „A Life (Black &
White)" versetzt den Ausstellungsbesucher in eine Installation, die zugleich eine Performance ist, eine Perfoman-
ce mit „kunstfremden" Akteuren, zwei handwerklichen
Anstreichern (oder Anstreicherinnen). In steter Folge
überziehen sie die Wände mit weißer beziehungsweise
schwarzer Farbe, wobei immer eine Hälfte des Raumes hell
und die andere dunkel ist. Weiß wird also über Schwarz ge-
legt, Schwarz über Weiß und dann wieder Weiß über
Schwarz. Und das von morgens, wenn die Ausstellung öff-
net, bis abends, wenn sie geschlossen wird, in einem
gleichbleibenden Rhythmus, Tag für Tag, solange die Präsentation dauert, allein unterbrochen von festgelegten
kurzen Pausen.

Eine scheinbar sinnlose, da stets wiederholte Tätigkeit,
vergleichbar der vergeblichen Bemühung des mythischen
Sisyphos, den schweren Stein einen Berg hinaufzuwälzen.
Die immer wiederkehrende Handlung, bei der ein zielge-
richtetes Ende und ein Sinn nicht erkennbar sind, entspricht letztendlich der Absurdität des unentwegten
menschlichen Bemühens im Angesicht der eigenen End-
lichkeit, des Todes. Sie erscheint als Bild des Lebens, als
habhafte Metapher für die Vergeblichkeit alles menschlichen Tuns und zugleich als Symbol für den ewigen Kreis-
lauf der Natur von Werden und Vergehen.

Solakov steht mit dieser Arbeit in der philosophischen
Tradition des Absurden, wie es besonders eindringlich
Samuel Beckett, Buster Keaton oder Charlie Chaplin dar-
stellen. Und wie bei den klassischen Slapstik-Meistern lie-
gen auch bei dem bildenden Künstler Tragik und ironischer
Humor eng beieinander.

Der Untertitel des Werkes „Black & White" führt den
erfahrenen Kunstbetrachter auf eine weitere Assoziations-
Fährte. Galt nicht lange Zeit (und gilt auch heute noch

*Well, I thought as I walked through a room at the preview
to the Venice Biennial 2001 where the walls were being painted,
I suppose they aren't ready yet. Nevertheless, I remained
standing by the exit and looked around. A man in working
clothes was whitewashing, opposite him a different man was
applying black paint to the wall – both quiet and concentra-
ted in the empty room, the middle of which was occupied by
no more than a few paint pots and the painters' equipment.
Finally, I discovered a written notice – "A Life (Black & White)",
transporting the exhibition visitor into an installation which
is simultaneously a performance, a performance with actors
"alien to art"; two painters and decorators. Steadily and continually, they cover the walls with white or black paint, where-
by one half of the room always remains bright, one half dark.
So white is painted over black, black over white and then white
over black again... from the morning when the exhibition is
opened to the evening when it is closed, with this regular rhy-
thm, day after day, as long as the presentation lasts, the only
interruption being short, planned breaks.*

*It is an apparently senseless activity – since it is constantly
repeated – one comparable with the vain labours of the
mythical Sisyphus as he rolled his heavy stone up the mountain. The constantly recurring activity, in which no purposeful
end and no meaning may be recognised, ultimately corresponds
to the absurdity of man's uninterrupted efforts in face of his
own finite nature; in face of death. It is manifest as an image
of life, as a tangible metaphor for the vanity of all human
activity, and at the same time it symbolises nature's eternal
cycle of birth and death.*

*This work places Solakov in the philosophical tradition of
the absurd, which has been represented in an especially vivid
way by Samuel Beckett, Buster Keaton or Charlie Chaplin. As
in the case of these classical masters of slapstick, the fine
artist also sees the proximity of tragedy and ironical humour.*

*The subtitle of the work, "Black & White", leads the ex-
perienced art viewer along an additional associative track.
Was the „White Cube" not viewed – for a long time (and in
many places still today) – as the sacrosanct exhibition space
of the modern age, as an optimal requirement meaning that a
work's spiritual element could be emphasised in a purist manner?
And a new cult space, the "Black Box", entered the art world
with the new media. This box, painted completely black and*

vielerorts) der „White Cube" als das sakrosankte Ausstellungsgehäuse der Moderne, als optimale Voraussetzung dafür, das Geistige eines Werkes puristisch hervortreten zu lassen? Mit den neuen Medien zog ein zweiter Kultraum, die „Black Box", in die Kunstwelt ein. Das gänzlich schwarz gestrichene, zuerst meist als eng und muffig erinnerte Gehäuse bot den technisch oft unzulänglichen Videofilmen der Anfangszeit sowie stockenden Diaprojektionen erste Auftritte.

Das sich so lapidar darbietende sinnlich-räumliche Werk „A Life" bietet also vielfältige gedanklich-assoziative Ansätze, die zu zentralen Themen des Künstlers führen.

Die „Art World" mit ihrem Kult um „Meisterwerke" und Sammler, mit ihren Kuratoren, Museumsdirektoren, den Fragen musealer Präsentation und Vermittlung reflektiert der Bulgare seit Mitte der neunziger Jahre in zahlreichen Installationen.

Aus der Sicht des „naiven" Berichterstatters stellt er z.B. 1994 den „Collector of Art" vor – ein afrikanischer Buschmann versammelt mit großer Leidenschaft in seiner Hütte Hauptwerke der westlichen Moderne, die nach den Gesetzen des angeblich ortsüblichen Tauschhandels, z.B. gegen Kokosnüsse, erworben hat (s. S. 73) – oder 1994 „Mr.Curator, please" (s. S. 72), wo sieben ehrwürdige Meister der klassischen Kunstgeschichte, bzw. ihre Geister, mit einem jungen Kunstvermittler um einen Auftrag streiten. Die strenge Kunstideologie der Moderne konterkariert Solakov 2001 auch in „A (not so) White Cube", indem er Ritzen in den weißen Wänden des Ausstellungsraumes mit miniaturhaft kleinen Schriften und Zeichnungen füllt (s. S. 49).

In „Thirteen (maybe)" betätigt sich Solakov 1998 selbst als (Gast-)Kurator. Die Archäologische Schausammlung eines Museums erhält durch seine Einfügung von Gegenständen und akustischen Klängen eine neue Gewichtung: Was wird wann und warum als wertvoll erklärt? Bereits sechs Jahre zuvor hatte „The Artist As Curator" aus Fundstücken ein überbordendes „Market"-Ensemble zusammengetragen.

Die scheinbar einfachen und heiteren Erzählungen aus der Welt der Kunst basieren auf deren scharfsinniger Analyse. Erst vor diesem Hintergrund erschließt sich der ganze surreale Reiz der phantasievollen und assoziationsreichen Erfindungen, ihre Intelligenz und ihr subversiver Humor.

Solakov hat sich für die Kunst als seine Form der Weltaneignung entschieden. So handeln die Installationen und die begleitenden Künstlerbücher immer auch von ihm, von seinen Leben als freier Künstler in dem komplizierten

usually recalled as narrow and stuffy, offered the first scenes for early, often technically inadequate video films and faltering slide projections.

The sensory, spatial work "A Life", therefore – which is presented in such a succinct way – offers a range of intellectually associative starting points leading us to the artist's central themes.

Since the mid-nineties, in numerous installations the Bulgarian has reflected upon the "art world" – with its cult surrounding "masterpieces" and collectors, with its curators, museum directors, and with questions of presentation and mediation in museums.

In 1994, for example, he presented the "Collector of Art" from the viewpoint of a "naïve" reporter – an African Bushman passionately collects important works of modern western art in his hut, supposedly acquired according to the traditions of local trade, in exchange for coconuts for example (see page 73) – or "Mr. Curator, please" (1994, see page 72) in which seven honoured masters of classical art history, or rather their ghosts, compete for a contract with a young art agent. Solakov also counteracted the strict art ideology of the modern age in "A (not so) White Cube" (2001), in which he filled gaps in the white walls of the exhibition room with miniature lettering and drawings (see page 49).

In "Thirteen (maybe)", dated 1998, Solakov himself acted as a (guest) curator. The archaeological display collection of a museum was given a new emphasis by his introduction to it of objects and sounds: what is declared valuable, when, and why? Six years earlier, "The Artist as Curator" had already assembled an overflowing "market" from found objects.

These apparently simple and cheerful narratives from the world of art are based on sharp-witted analysis. It is only before this background that the full surreal attraction of his highly imaginative and associative inventions is revealed – demonstrating their intelligence and subversive humour.

Solakov has decided in favour of art as a means of appropriating the world. So the installations and the accompanying artists' books are always concerned with the artist himself, with his life as a fine artist within the complicated system of a global "art world" located between east and west. In addition, the works reflect a general thoughtfulness regarding human existence; they are about expectations, longings and needs.

Precise observation and ironic reflection on this observation can create distance. Solakov is probably referring to himself, therefore, when he introduces the artist in "The Thief of Art" – an extensive story about an art theft from 1994/96 – as a

A Life (Black & White)
1998-2001; schwarze und weiße Farbe, zwei Arbeiter/Maler, die die Wände des Ausstellungsraums kontinuierlich schwarz und weiß bemalen. Die Tätigkeit wird Tag für Tag, für die Gesamtdauer der Ausstellung (31 Tage) ausgeführt/*black and white paint, two workers/painters constantly repainting the walls of the exhibition space in black and white for the entire duration of the exhibition (31 days), day after day (following each other)*; variable Dimensionen/*dimensions variable*; „L 'Autre moitie de l'Europe," Galerie National du Jeu de Paume, Paris, 2000. Courtesy der Künstler/*the artist*.

System einer globalen „Artworld" zwischen Ost und West. Darüber hinaus spiegeln die Werke ein generelles Nachdenken über die menschliche Existenz, über Erwartungen, Sehnsüchte und Nöte.

Genaue Beobachtung und deren ironische Reflektion können Distanz schaffen. So spricht Solakov wohl über sich, wenn er den Künstler in „The Thief of Art", in einer umfassenden Geschichte mit einem Kunstdiebstahl, 1994/96 als „Balcan Barbarian from Bulgaria" einführt, und von dem Dieb, einem Furcht erregenden Yeti, zum Schluß raten läßt: „You should never, ever touch the art world again!" (s. S. 72). Als spöttischer Kommentar zu seinen (geheimen) Wünschen und zu denen der Kollegen, der zugleich über das bisher von ihm Erreichte Rechenschaft ablegt, arrangiert Solakov 1996 zu gediegenen Ölgemälden transformierte Photos seiner Werke in quasi barocker Hängung zu „Desires" mit dem Untertitel „The extreme desire of the avantgarde artist his art to look in classical way".

„A Life (Black & White)" wirkt formal strenger als die früheren Arbeiten, die vielgliedriger und stärker erzählerisch strukturiert sind. Diese fügen sich aus ganz unterschiedlichen Teilen wie gezeichneten und photographierten Bildern, aus Stoffen und Gegenständen aller Art zu Ensembles zusammen und werden durch handgeschriebene Texte des Künstlers kommentiert. Solakov verbindet hier zum ersten Mal Installation mit Performance, er verzichtet auf jeden schriftlichen Zusatz. Damit kommen eine neue Ebene körperlich sinnlicher Erfahrung und das Phänomen Zeit in sein Werk. Dem konzeptuellen Charakter der Arbeit entspricht, daß Solakov sie als 5er-Auflage definiert: Sie kann ohne seine direkte Mitwirkung nach detaillierten schriftlichen Vorgaben realisiert werden.

Solakovs Biennale-Beitrag von 2001 ist wohl sein bekanntestes Werk, auch weil es inzwischen mehrmals verwirklicht wurde. Daß vier Installationen zwar in unterschiedlich großen Räumen und unterschiedlich lange, aber doch partiell zeitgleich in Venedig, München, Glasgow und Dublin durchgeführt wurden, regte den Künstler zu einer zusammenfassenden Arbeit an. An diesem Tag nahmen vier Filmer zur gleichen Stunde an den jeweiligen Orten die Performance auf, Solakov filmt sich parallel selbst, wie er in seinem Stockholmer Atelier zweihändig mit weißer und schwarzer Farbe einen Karton bemalt. Als Videoprojektion können die fünf Ereignisse nun in einem nachvollzogen werden („20.10.2001", 2002, Galerie Erna Hécey, Luxemburg). Solakov führt so auch im Medium Film die Verknüpfung von Arbeit und Leben fort und läßt in dieser Virtualität die Komponente Zeit noch deutlicher hervortreten.

Brigitte Reinhardt

"Balkan Barbarian from Bulgaria." At the end, this artist is also advised by the thief, a frightening Yeti: "You should never, ever touch the art world again!" (see page 72). In 1996, as a mocking commentary on his own (secret) wishes and those of his colleagues, at the same time giving an account of his achievements to date, Solakov hung a quasi baroque arrangement of photos transformed into tasteful oil paintings to create "Desires" with the subtitle "The extreme desire of the avantgarde artist his art to look in a classical way."

With respect to form, "A Life (Black & White)" makes a stricter impression than the earlier works, which have more parts and are structured in a more narrative way. They are assembled from completely different components such as drawn and photographed images, cloth and objects of all kinds, whilst hand-written texts by the artist comment upon them. Here Solakov combines installation with performance for the first time, rejecting any written supplement. In this way, a new level of physical, sensual experience and the phenomenon of time enter into his work. The fact that Solakov defines the work as an edition of 5 corresponds to its conceptual character: without his direct participation, it can still be realised by following detailed, written instructions.

By now, Solakov's contribution to the Biennial has probably become his best-known work, since it has also been realised several times. The fact that four installations had been realised – in different sized rooms and for different lengths of time, but partially simultaneously in Venice, Munich, Glasgow and Dublin – stimulated the artist to produce a summarizing work. On that day, between 5 and 6 p.m., four cameramen recorded the performance simultaneously at each of the venues, whilst at the same time Solakov filmed himself in his Stockholm studio painting over a piece of cardboard with two hands – one with black paint the other with white. The five events can now be followed as one in a video projection ("20.10.2001", 2002, Galerie Erna Hécey, Luxembourg). In this way, Solakov also continues to link art and life using the medium of film, making the component of time appear more clearly still in this virtual sphere.

A Life (Black & White)
1998-2001; schwarze und weiße Farbe, zwei Arbeiter/Maler, die die Wände des Ausstellungsraums kontinuierlich schwarz und weiß bemalen. Die Tätigkeit wird Tag für Tag, für die Gesamtdauer der Ausstellung ausgeführt/*black and white paint, two workers/painters constantly repainting the walls of the exhibition space in black and white for the entire duration of the exhibition, day after day (following each other); variable* Dimensionen/*dimensions variable.*
1. „Marking the Territory," Irish Museum of Modern Art, Dublin, 2001 (3 Tage/ days).
2. „Total Object Complete with Missing Parts," Tramway, Glasgow, 2001 (53 Tage/days).
3. „Loop – Alles auf Anfang," Kunsthalle der Hypo-Kulturstiftung, München, 2001 (52 Tage/days).
Courtesy der Künstler/*the artist.*

vorhergehende Seite/*previous page:*
A Life (Black & White)
1998-2001; schwarze und weiße Farbe, zwei Arbeiter/Maler, die die Wände des Ausstellungsraums kontinuierlich schwarz und weiß bemalen. Die Tätigkeit wird Tag für Tag, für die Gesamtdauer der Ausstellung uasgeführt (fünf Monate)/*black and white paint; two workers/ painters constantly repainting the walls of the exhibition space in black and white for the entire duration of the exhibition (five months), day after day (following each other); variable* Dimensionen/*dimensions variable;* „Plateau of Humankind," 49. Biennale Venedig, 2001/*49th Venice Biennale, 2001;* Collection Susan and Lewis Manilow, Chicago; Sammlung Hauser und Wirth, St. Gallen.
Courtesy der Künstler/*the artist.*

Vitiligo People #2 2001; farbfester Filzstift auf Lambdaprint /*permanent felt pen on a lambda print*;
120 x 150 cm; Collection Laura Pecci.

Vitiligo People
2001; Wandtext, farbfester Filzstift auf
Lambdaprints, eine Serie von 7/*wall text,
permanent felt pen on lambda prints, a series of 7*;
je/*each* 120 x 150 cm; Installation view –
Galleria Laura Pecci, Milano, 2001.
Courtesy Galleria Laura Pecci *und/and the artist*.

FROM the "WISE" SERIES #1.

SEVEN WISE MEN with different backgrounds are trying to figure out if they should unify themselves temporarily in order to kill the everyday-life kind of little insignificant thought that appeared incidentally atop one of their heads or if they just should leave that little intruder to die on its own.

CORAK '2001

Wise #4
2001; Tusche (sepia, schwarz und weiß) laviert/*sepia, black and white ink and wash on paper*; 19 x 28 cm.
Courtesy Galerie Arndt & Partner und/*and* der Künstler/*the artist*.

"**Destroyed Public Sculpture**" – At first glance, this sounds very bad...bad for the artist, whose work is going to be destroyed, bad for the institution on whose property the artwork is located, bad for the local community which is the actual owner and finally...bad for the author of this barbarian project (me) who apparently doesn't have anymore fresh ideas except this one: to use someone else's oeuvre to express himself in a nasty way. This may be bad for another reason too – in order to fulfill this project, the artist (me) had to obtain permission for this, in general, illegal act from the artwork's owner, the Police Department of the City of Arnhem and in such a case, where exactly is the supposedly brave and charming anarchical artistic gesture? Too many bad things.

Destroyed Public Sculpture
2001; zerstörte Kopie von einem Teil einer Skulptur im öffentlichen Raum „Citizens" (von Ubo Scheffer, 1970), früherer Standort vor dem Hauptpolizeirevier, Arnhem, Niederlande / destroyed replica of a part of a public sculpture called "Citizens" (created by Ubo Scheffer, 1970), situated in front of the Police Headquarters, Arnhem, The Netherlands; „Locus/Focus," Sonsbeek'9, Arnhem, 2001.
Courtesy Sonsbeek'9 und / and der Künstler / the artist.

What I will say in my defense is that I would only like to deliver with all due respect to the author of the "Citizens" sculptural group and to its owner – The Police Department – a tiny little message in the public space of the city of Arnhem – a message which says nothing more than: "Are you sure, my dear viewer, that you like the way you live? If you do, then please get furious with the bloody Bulgarian who dares to take down part of this paid for with-your-tax-money sculpture; but if you don't like so much the way your existence goes (no matter who you are – rich or poor, healthy or ill, a nice guy or a bad one) then, perhaps, you will understand my gesture – I don't like my way of living either."

I hope that there are not so many happy and self-satisfied people in the world.

Nedko Solakov
February, 2001

Edited by Geneva Anderson

CAUSE OF the jetlag I FEEL tired and sleepy.
I have no more ideas what to do
ith these nice things (above)

you have any
a what to do
th them (what
tories, I mean)
ease contact
he floor manager
onsible for fresh
as.

st of the stuff
ilable to play with.
r wars creature - 1p.
ange flying animal - 1p.
dead ugly bastard
out 9 snakes
e wolf man
e mummy
e hunchback of N.D.
e creature from
black lagoon
rankenstein
Japanese sexy female
artoon warrior
e invisible man
frogs.

A (not so) White Cube
2001; mixed-media, fast unsichtbar/*mixed, almost
invisible, media*; variable Dimensionen/*dimensions
variable*; P.S.1 Special Projects Program, P.S.1
Contemporary Art Center, New York.
Courtesy der Künstler/*the artist* und/*and* P.S.1.

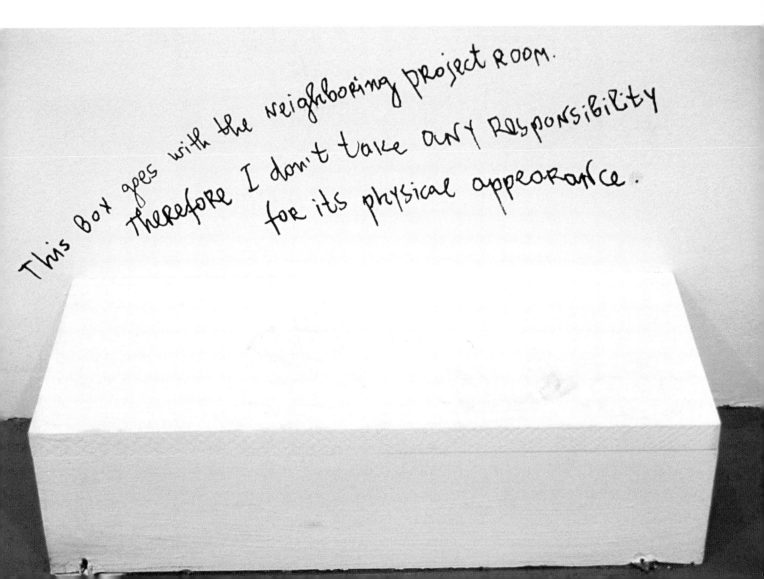

Good News, Bad News
1998-2000; Kinderspielzeug, örtliche Sex-
werbung, Glas, Wasser, Würfel, künstliche
Blume, Filzstift, handgeschriebene Texte auf
Papier und Stein, 12 Scheinwerfer / *children's
toys, local sex advertisement, glass, water, dice,
artificial flower, felt pen, handwritten texts on
paper and stone, 12 spotlights; variable Dimensionen / dimensions variable; Aus „Stories 1"
Einzelausstellung, Center for Contemporary
Art, Ujazdowski Castle, Warsaw, 2000 / From
"Stories 1" one-person exhibition, Center for Contemporary Art, Ujazdowski Castle, Warsaw, 2000.
Courtesy der Künstler / the artist.*

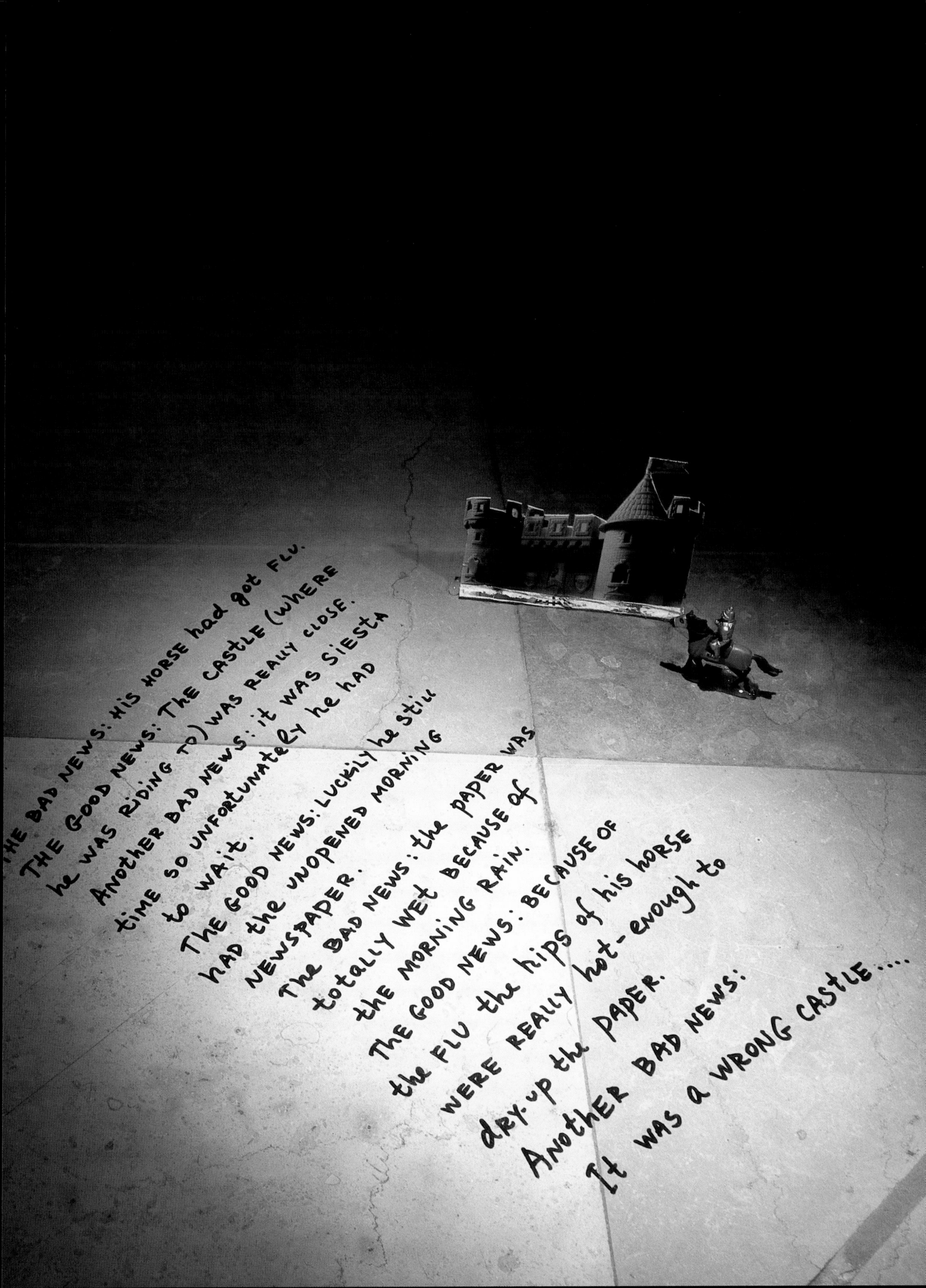

THE BAD NEWS: HIS HORSE had got FLU.

THE GOOD NEWS: THE CASTLE (WHERE
he WAS RIDING TO) WAS REALLY CLOSE.

Another BAD NEWS: it WAS SIESTA
time so unfortunately he had
to wait.

THE GOOD NEWS: Luckily he still
had the unopened morning
NEWSPAPER.

The BAD NEWS: the PAPER WAS
totally WET BECAUSE OF
the MORNING RAIN.

THE GOOD NEWS: BECAUSE OF
the FLU the hips of his horse
were REALLY hot-enough to
dry-up the PAPER.

Another BAD NEWS:

It WAS a WRONG CASTLE.....

....I am a poor bisexual form, my male origin is going square and my female one keeps on baroquing. Sometimes they change places and I get totally confused because of the new taxes I have to pay....

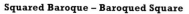

Squared Baroque – Baroqued Square
2000; vergoldete, geschnitzte Holzobjekte, Terrakotta-Figuren von Mitjo Solakov, Murmel, Kau-gummi, farbfester Filzstift, Texte, diskret plaziert unter die Dauerausstellungsstücke des Ikonen-Museums, Frankfurt am Main/*gilded carved wooden objects, terracotta figures created by Mitjo Solakov, marble, chewing gum, permanent felt pen, texts, all placed in discreet ways among the permanent exhibits of Ikonen-Museum, Frankfurt am Main;* variable Dimensionen/*dimensions variable.* Gemeinschaftsprojekt mit Portikus/*A joint project with Portikus.*
Courtesy der Künstler/*the artist*, des Ikonen-Museums und/*and* Portikus.

UNPROPER, UNGERMAN!

The Disappointed River

My dear wanderer, please take a look at FULDA River (on your left). Doesn't she seem kind of disappointed, even miserable, with her waters trickling so slowly? Yes, she is and I'll tell you why.

It so happens that her beloved letters F, U, L, D and A were totally neglected during the merger with the WERRA River. As you see, these letters are missing from the new river's name, WESER. The poor FULDA was only given the right of proxy representation in the new word, so she chose the letter S, which replaced one of the double R's from WERRA. Why S? The bends in the S reminded the obviously sentimental letters F, U, L and D of the cute curves at the FULDA's source, up where those letters are still little babbling brooks.

The sensitive FULDA River couldn't help but feel fated by this injustice – she had been working so hard all these centuries – apparently for nothing! And in order to gain a form of spiritual compensation, the FULDA began to help merchants who were required to pay horrible staple rights and stacking taxes for all the goods and merchandise entering the City of Muenden. These awful taxes, by the way, went mainly to building elegant houses on the competitor WERRA's banks. So, the FULDA smuggled some goods over her waters – a small, but calming, act of retribution.

The two A letters from FULDA and WERRA were not satisfied with this merger either. Imagine! the first letter in all alphabets being neglected in such a brutal way! However, a small bonus was offered to them as well. An arrangement was made so that these two A letters would appear as the beginning of the name of a beautiful German city, somewhere West....

Edited by Geneva Anderson

The Disappointed River
2000; Fulda, Werra und Weser, Touristen Weser Sandstein, bronzene Tafel, Text/ *Fulda, Werra and Weser rivers, tourists, Weser sandstone, bronze plate, text;* 120 x 85 x 90 cm; „3 Räume – 3 Flüsse," Hann. Münden, 2000. Courtesy der Künstler/*the artist.*

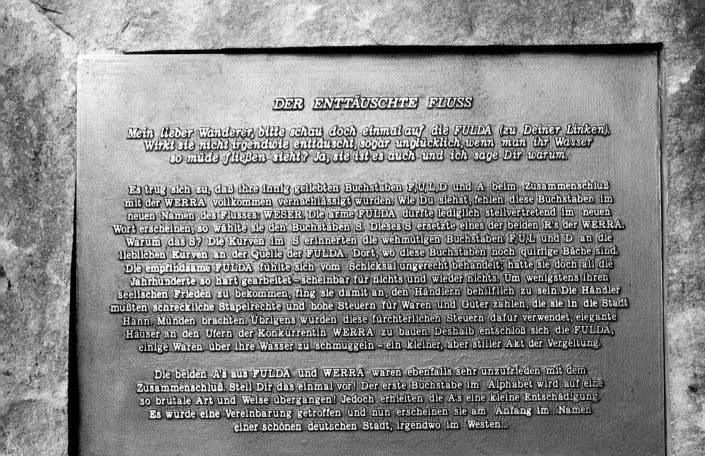

DER ENTTÄUSCHTE FLUSS

Mein lieber Wanderer, bitte schau doch einmal auf die FULDA (zu Deiner Linken). Wirkt sie nicht irgendwie enttäuscht, sogar unglücklich, wenn man ihr Wasser so müde fließen sieht? Ja, sie ist es auch und ich sage Dir warum.

Es trug sich zu, daß ihre innig geliebten Buchstaben F, U, L, D und A beim Zusammenschluß mit der WERRA vollkommen vernachlässigt wurden. Wie Du siehst, fehlen diese Buchstaben im neuen Namen des Flusses: WESER. Die arme FULDA durfte lediglich stellvertretend im neuen Wort erscheinen, so wählte sie den Buchstaben S. Dieses S ersetzte eines der beiden R's der WERRA. Warum das S? Die Kurven im S erinnerten die wehmütigen Buchstaben F, U, L und D an die lieblichen Kurven an der Quelle der FULDA. Dort, wo diese Buchstaben noch quirlige Bäche sind. Die empfindsame FULDA fühlte sich vom Schicksal ungerecht behandelt; hatte sie doch all die Jahrhunderte so hart gearbeitet – scheinbar für nichts und wieder nichts. Um wenigstens ihren seelischen Frieden zu bekommen, fing sie damit an, den Händlern behilflich zu sein. Die Händler mußten schreckliche Stapelrechte und hohe Steuern für Waren und Güter zahlen, die sie in die Stadt Hann. Münden brachten. Übrigens wurden diese fürchterlichen Steuern dafür verwendet, elegante Häuser an den Ufern der Konkurrentin WERRA zu bauen. Deshalb entschloß sich die FULDA, einige Waren über ihre Wasser zu schmuggeln – ein kleiner, aber stiller Akt der Vergeltung.

Die beiden A's aus FULDA und WERRA waren ebenfalls sehr unzufrieden mit dem Zusammenschluß. Stell Dir das einmal vor! Der erste Buchstabe im Alphabet wird auf eine so brutale Art und Weise übergangen! Jedoch erhielten die A's eine kleine Entschädigung. Es wurde eine Vereinbarung getroffen und nun erscheinen sie am Anfang im Namen einer schönen deutschen Stadt, irgendwo im Westen...

EL BULGARO – THE SENSATIONAL DISCOVERY

As disclosed recently, during El Greco's time, a no less gifted artist lived. El Bulgaro was his name and his paintings and drawings by comparison to the Great Greco's happened to show much more natural-looking people – not the dancing worm type of elongated figures but mighty, kind of flattened-out, stern, but still cute, guys. Who was this person? Why hasn't anyone heard anything about El Bulgaro?

It is still a secret. Due to very complicated circumstances, it was not possible to disclose his oeuvre before the year 2000. Even now, when it is appropriate to do so, it is still too dangerous to exhibit El Bulgaro's originals (that is why, dear connoisseur, you may have a glimpse only at mediocre recent copies/replicas of part of El Bulgaro's work.) It seems that a heavy discussion of this „discovery" will take place over the next decade.

Special attention must be paid to one of the possible explanations of the phenomenal El Bulgaro's existence (kept for centuries in deep secret). There is too much hard-to-ignore evidence that El Greco himself was hiding behind El Bulgaro's personality. The production of all these elongated, slimy, unhealthy figures all day long, day after day, commission after commission, apparently placed an enormous burden on El Greco's psyche. Most probably, during the full moon, on those Toledo nights, the famous Greek would wake up acting like a lunatic, not capable of realizing what he was doing, and led by his subconscious impulses, he would enter his studio again (or another – still unknown, room) and start painting these mighty, natural-looking men and women, bites from daily life.

According to another (not yet publicly-disclosed) document, El Greco's second ego came from one of his grandmothers who adventurously moved to the island of Crete from Southern Bulgaria (which was at that time under Turkish occupation). It seems that this Bulgarian grandmother put a fateful mark over little Domenikos. The Bulgarian seed worked deeply in his mind during his early years in Crete, Venice, Rome, Madrid and finally it exploded in an unexpected, unpredictable way in Toledo. On some of the surviving works, there is the signature "El Bulgaro." Finally, the artist felt free to disclose his identity. The Bulgarian ego guided him through full moon nights when he sought spiritual balance. The limelight on El Greco's widely-acclaimed glorious altarpieces and official portraits found its counterpart in the moonlight illuminating the weird El Bulgaro's modest but no less honest little paintings.

An incidental witness of these activities happened to be one of the house servants who immediately reported to the family. The folks were horrified and at once called for the family doctor who performed an extensive treatment on El Greco's body (secretly, of course. The same doctor observed that a possible reason for El Greco's moonlight walks might be an overdose of the hot chocolate that he normally drank in the late afternoon. The drink was pretty new at that time, a fresh arrival from the new overseas provinces and therefore it still had not been examined properly). The family council decided to keep this second behavior of the artist a secret. The scandal that certainly would have arisen in the society of potential clients was something that could not be risked. Not to mention, the Inquisition authorities, even in those times, didn't like Bulgarians so much. Therefore, the already painted works were locked away in a safe secret place and the doctor treated the Maestro with a short series of highly-advanced hypnotism sessions (during which appeared the details of his shameful Bulgarian origin). The servant who witnessed El Bulgaro/El Greco in action was kicked out of the house. Unfortunately, in order to have some retribution, that dishonest man sold the idea for the peculiar co-existence of a Tall, Slimy, Elongated, Noble figure and a Flattened out, Mighty (fat) guy to a relatively unpopular writer named Cervantes or something.

And so on and so forth – a small part of this unbelievable story is before you. Take a look and think about it.....

Nedko Solakov
January 2000, Sofia

Edited by Geneva Anderson

El Bulgaro
2000; mixed-media (sehr komplex), Texte/*complicated mixed media, texts;*
variable Dimensionen/*dimensions variable;* Installation view –
Galerie Arndt & Partner, ARCO Project Rooms, Madrid, 2000.
Courtesy der Künstler/*the artist* und/*and* Galerie Arndt & Partner, Berlin.

Aus/From **El Bulgaro: Don Pedro**
2000; Acrylfarbe auf Holz/*acrylic on wood*; 33 x 25 x 3 cm.
Private Sammlung, Mailand/*Private Collection, Milano.*

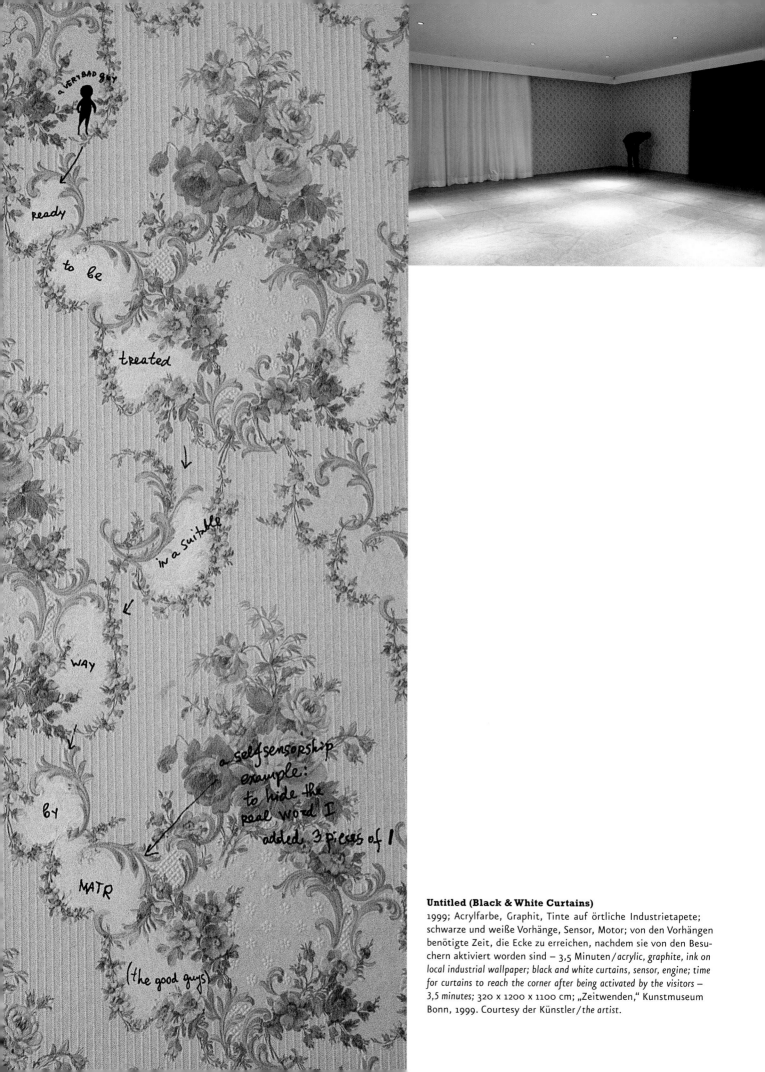

a VERY BAD guy
ready
to be
treated
in a suitable
WAY
by
a selfsensorship
example:
to hide the
real word I
added 3 pieces of I
MATR
(the good guys)

Untitled (Black & White Curtains)
1999; Acrylfarbe, Graphit, Tinte auf örtliche Industrietapete; schwarze und weiße Vorhänge, Sensor, Motor; von den Vorhängen benötigte Zeit, die Ecke zu erreichen, nachdem sie von den Besuchern aktiviert worden sind – 3,5 Minuten/*acrylic, graphite, ink on local industrial wallpaper; black and white curtains, sensor, engine; time for curtains to reach the corner after being activated by the visitors – 3,5 minutes*; 320 x 1200 x 1100 cm; „Zeitwenden," Kunstmuseum Bonn, 1999. Courtesy der Künstler/*the artist*.

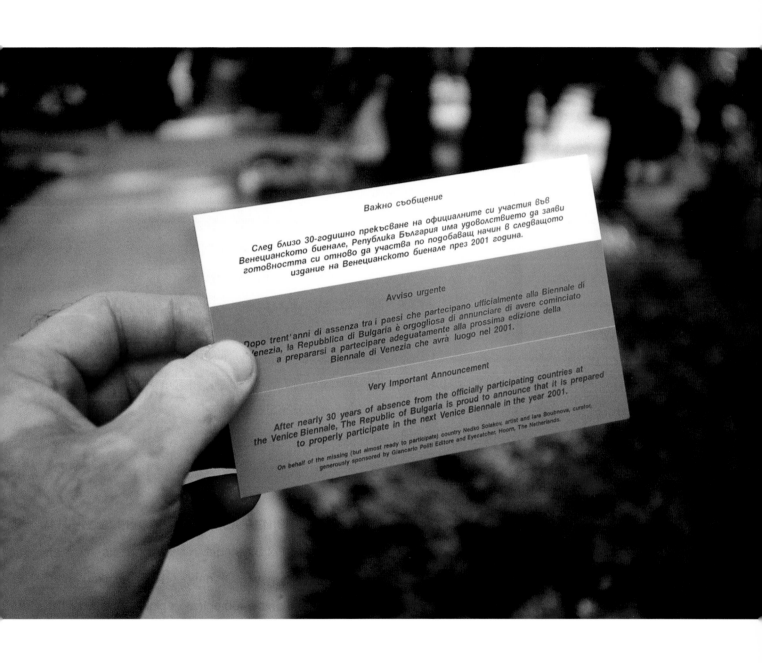

Announcement
1999; Mitteilung – auf 15.000 Postkarten und T-Shirts aufgedruckt;
Offizielle Beteiligung Bulgariens an 48. Biennale Venedig, 1999/
a message printed on 15.000 postcards and T-shirts;
Official participation of Bulgaria in the 48th Venice Biennale, 1999.
Courtesy der Künstler/*the artist,* ICA und/*and* ATA, Sofia.

Quotations

1999; ausgestopfte, schwarze, samtene Einführungsstriche um ein gestiftetes japanisches Gemälde (riesig und nicht entfernbar)/ *stuffed black velvet quotation marks around a donated Japanese painting (huge and non-removable)*; variable Dimensionen/*dimensions variable* „Locally Interested," 1999, ICA Sofia im Eingangsbereich des Museum for Foreign Art, Sofia/*ICA Sofia in the halls of the Museum for Foreign Art, Sofia*. Courtesy der Künstler/*the artist* und/*and* Museum for Foreign Art, Sofia.

1999-2000; ausgestopfte, schwarze, samtene Einführungsstriche um ein nicht entfernbares Michetti Gemälde/*stuffed black velvet quotation marks around a non-removable Michetti painting*; variable Dimensionen/*dimensions variable* „Premio Michetti 2000," Fondazione Michetti, Francavilla al Mare, Chieti, Italien/*Italy*. Courtesy der Künstler/*the artist* und/*and* Fondazione Michetti.

1999; ausgestopfte, schwarze, samtene Einführungsstriche um ein „art shop" im Eingangsbereich des Museum for Foreign Art, Sofia/ *stuffed black velvet quotation marks around an 'art shop' situated at the entrance hall of the Museum for Foreign Art, Sofia*; variable Dimensionen/ *dimensions variable*; „Locally Interested," 1999, ICA Sofia in the halls of the Museum for Foreign Art, Sofia. Courtesy der Künstler/*the artist*.

Floor
1999; verschiedene Reißzwecken und Stifte, an den Museumsboden gepinnt/*various push- and map pins over the museum parquet floor*; variable Dimensionen/*dimensions variable* „Locally Interested," 1999, ICA Sofia im Eingangsbereich des Museum for Foreign Art, Sofia/*Locally Interested," 1999, ICA Sofia in the halls of the Museum for Foreign Art, Sofia.* Courtesy der Künstler/*the artist.*

1996; verschiedene Reißzwecken und Stifte, in den Museumsboden gepinnt/*various push- and map pins over the museum parquet floor,* variable Dimensionen/ *dimensions variable;* „The Sense of Order," Museum of Modern Art, Ljubljana, 1996. Courtesy der Künstler/*the artist* und/ *and* Museum of Modern Art, Ljubljana.

1. (left wing)

"Dear passenger, somewhere down over there, behind the second mountain, on the left bank of a tiny river, is a little hill. In that little hill there is a little hole and in that hole lives a little mole. Frankly, she would love to be in your place right now – almost 10,000 meters above the ground...."

2. (left wing)

"Don't worry. Everything will be fine. You will make it. You will find the money...."

3. (left wing)

"This very wing has two edges – a leading edge and a trailing edge. They are brothers (or something). Sometimes the trailing edge gets paranoid. „I could never be a leading one!" he worries. Luckily, his brother is capable of calming him down: "My dear, I would never exist if I didn't have your support. Have you ever known a leading edge to fly alone?"

4. (left wing)

"Under this very wing there is a very small rain drop hanging on to the silver metal....somewhere close to the wheel.... She is very happy. Why? Because later on she intends to drop down on that (sometimes snowy) mountain where her beloved cousins live. They are some of the best snowflakes in the World."

5. (left wing)

"The same text appears on the right wing too....but you better check."

6. (left wing)

"Dear passenger, would you try to look at the sky above you – yes, exactly above you .... at that place where the not so deep blue becomes a very deep blue and where the very deep blue transits into the Universe's deepest colour.... If you can make it, you will be able to see a beautiful scene – a sleeping extraterrestrial postman (maybe they use another word for the postman – who knows?). He is waiting for the nearest cable TV satellite to pass by. He missed the last episode of his soap and is waiting to get the story first hand...."

1. (right wing)

"My dear passenger, did you see the silver dollar hidden at the very bottom of the compartment above your head? That's correct – it happens to be under your hand luggage. Take it later! It's yours."

2. (right wing)

"Dear passenger, can you see that little cloud on the right... so young and relatively small. He wants so much to be like the Big Mighty Guys (close to the horizon)... but, for the time being, he can't and that is why he is a bit sad.... but not so sad because his responsibility for the Atmosphere's image is not so big either...."

3. (right wing)

"Actually the aileron closest to you would very much like to say "Hello!" and to greet you by waving up and down three times. But his mother, the cockpit, has rules. He will greet you later while landing."

4. (right wing)

"Hi! Yes, it's me who just said "Hi!"

4. (right wing, closer)

"If you keep staring at these very letters, be sure, you will fall asleep very, very soon.... just look at them. Look at us....read us again and again.... again and again...and your eyes are closing.... the friendly sound of the engine is caressing your body.... you are already sleeping although your eyes might be still open.... sleeping....and the beautiful dream which disappeared so mysteriously this morning will visit you again...."

5. (right wing)

"The same text appears on the left wing too.... but you better check"

6. (right wing)

"Lucky you! The most beautiful crew is in your plane."

6. (right wing, closer)

"If a housefly (Musca domestica) could be an astronaut, do you think she could, using appropriate housefly astronaut equipment, reach our altitude?"

Edited by Geneva Anderson

On the Wing

1999-2000; 14 Texte auf den Tragflächen von sechs Boeings 737, Luxair/*14 texts on the wings of six Boeings 737, Luxair*; „Faiseurs d'histoires," Casino Luxembourg – Forum d'art contemporain, 1999. Courtesy der Künstler/*the artist* und/*and* Casino Luxembourg and Luxair.
Für „On the Wing" Lambda Printauflage, 12 Tafeln, insgesamt 120 x 160 cm/*for "On the Wing" lambda print edition, 12 panels, all together 120 x 160 cm* – Courtesy Galerie Georges-Philippe & Nathalie Vallois, Paris.

Saint Pipo (who instead of giving presents takes away the Christmas presents)
1998; mixed media auf Holz/*mixed media on wood*; 60 x 42 x 5 cm.
Courtesy der Künstler/*the artist* und/*and* Galerie arsFutura Zürich.

Aus / From **Wars – „The Poor Turtles Story"**
1997; Cibachrome; 50 x 70 cm; aus einer
Serie von 7 / from a series of 7.

Wars
1997; Gemälde, Zeichnungen, Cibachromes,
kleine, funktionierende Modelle von römischen
Wurfmaschinen, „The Dancing Knife" Videofilm,
Texte / paintings, drawings, cibachromes, small working
models of Roman catapults, "The Dancing Knife" video
film, texts; variable Dimensionen / dimensions variable;
Installation view – Galerie Erna Hécey, Luxembourg.
Courtesy Galerie Erna Hécey und /
and der Künstler / the artist.

Help Yourself (Russian Roulette)
1998; Zucker, Farbmittel, Mehl, Schokolade, Faltpapier, 7 Stück (in einem Stück befinden sich abgeschnittene Fingernägel des Künstlers)/*sugar, coloring agents, flour, chocolate, pleated paper, 7 pieces (the artist's clipped off nails inside one of them)*; je 5 x 5 x 5 cm. 7; Triennale der Kleinplastik, Stuttgart, 1998.
Courtesy der Künstler/*the artist.*

vorhergehende Seiten/*previous pages:*
Somewhere (under the tree)
1995-97; Textilien, PVC, Thermoplastik, Terrakotta, und Draht auf örtlichen Baumstämmen (die meisten Objekte wurden von dem Vater, der Frau und den Kindern des Künstlers gebaut)/*textile, PVC, thermoplastic, terracotta, and wire on local tree trunks (most of the objects made by the artist's father, wife and kids)*; variable Dimensionen/*dimensions variable*; Deitch Projects, New York, 1997.
Courtesy der Künstler/*the artist* und/*and* Deitch Projects.

The New Ones

1996; 5 Porträts, Öl auf Leinen, je 97 x 130 cm; 18 Skizzen, Tinte, Graphit auf Papier, je 9 x 13 cm bis 27 x 38 cm; vergoldete Rahmen, in „English red walls" gemalt, Text/*5 portraits, oil on linen, 97 x 130 cm each; 18 preparatory drawings, ink, graphite on paper, from 9 x 13 cm to 27 x 38 cm; gilded frames, walls painted in 'English red', text;* Variable Dimensionen/*dimensions variable;* „Inklusion: Exklusion," Künstlerhaus Graz, 1996.
Courtesy der Künstler/*the artist* und/*and* Steirischer Herbst.

DUST IMAGINE:

What would happen if I were to start to live as an ammonite, as a stuffed puck, as a rock crystal, as a snowflake, as the colour spectrum, as the material that this very wooden floor (on which you are now standing) is covered with....?

NORMALLY, EVERYBODY DREAMS to be "SOMEBODY ELSE": a famous actor, a BRAVE knight, a Rich hero....

I want to BE "a SOMETHING ELSE"— "something" which I know FROM MY OLD school books, FROM THE NATURAL HISTORY MUSEUMS' collections OR just from the inanimate NATURE.

Who KNOWS - MAYBE IN this case: with ME AS an AMMONITE, as a STUFFED DUCK, as a SNOWFLAKE....) I could ESTABLISH A MORE SUITABLE RELATIONSHIP with the SOCIETY around ME....

This is me, too...
1996; mixed (zuviel) media, alle Kostüme von Slava Nakovska entworfen und realisiert / mixed (too much) media, all costumes designed and executed by Slava Nakovska; variable Dimensionen / dimensions variable; Manifesta 1, Natural History Museum, Rotterdam, 1996.
Collection De Vleeshal, Middelburg, The Netherlands.

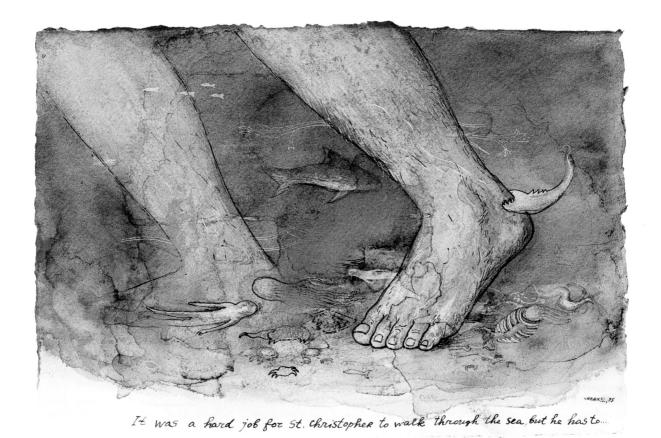

It was a hard job for St. christopher to walk through the sea, but he has to...

Version '92 in the collection of Monica von Senger, Zurich.

ABRAHAM REALLY WANTED VERY MUCH TO SACRIFICE SOMEBODY...

Aus/From Well-Known Stories
1992-1995; Tusche (sepia, schwarz und weiß) laviert; eine Reihe von 25 Zeichnungen/
sepia, black and white ink and wash on paper; a series of 25 drawings; je/each 19 x 28 cm.
Courtesy der Künstler/the artist.

Aus / From **The Truth (The Earth is Plane, the World is Flat)**
1992-95; „The Sailor's Tattoo", Cibachrome, 70 x 50 cm.
Courtesy der Künstler / *the artist*.

So, here it is:
SOMEBODY is STEALING SMALL WORKS OF ART
FROM FAMOUS PUBLIC AND PRIVATE COLLECTIONS..
DIRECTORS, CURATORS, COLLECTORS ARE HORRIFIED.

THE INSURANCE COMPANIES too....
ALL AROUND THE WORLD UNBELIEVABLE THEFTS
with the SAME HAND (PINCH) WRITTING —
NO BROKEN DOORS, NO SMASHED WALLS,
NO cut WINDOWS.... MYSTICALLY OPENED
VITRINES, COMPLETELY BLOCKED SECURITY SYSTEMS.

AND NOBODY SAW THE THIEF, NOBODY COULD GIVE
ANY LOGICAL INFORMATION ABOUT HIM OR HER....

Who is THIS GUY, who is THIS THIEF OF ART?

THE BiG FOOT (YETi)
OFCOURSE

The Thief of Art (Yeti, The Big Foot)
1995-96; Zeichnungen, Cornflakes, Gemälde, Kinderspielzeug, 2 Monitoren, 2 VHS-Spieler,
2 Videofilme, je ca. 15 Minuten; Texte auf verschiedenen Trägern; Geräusch von Meereswellen,
Rettungsboot, Kieselsteine, Originale von Warhol, Per Kirkeby, Kobra Künstler, Lego Spielzeug,
usw./drawings, cornflakes, paintings, children's toys, 2 monitors, 2 VHS players, 2 video films, app. 15 minutes
each; texts on various supports; ocean waves sound, rescue boat, pebbles, originals by Warhol, Per Kirkeby,
Kobra artist, Lego toy, etc.; variable Dimensionen/dimensions variable; Detail, „Scream," Arken Museum
of Modern Art, Copenhagen, 1996.
Courtesy der Künstler/the artist, Arken Museum of Modern Art und/and Yeti.

Mr. Curator, please....
1995; Computer, Monitor mit „running ghosts
screensaver" Programm; Telefon mit abgelegtem
Hörer und sich wiederholender Audiomitteilung;
Diaprojektor, 80 Dias, ständig im 1 Sekunden-
abstand laufend; Bücher zu den Werken von Bosch,
Breugel, Dürer, Leonardo, Michelangelo, Rubens
und Jan van Eyck; Pressematerial; Zeitschriften;
Dias in Plastikhefter; T-Shirt; eine Tasse kalten Kaf-
fees; Medikamente; Kugelschreiber; italienisches
Geld; eine Karte von Berlin; Schreibtischlampe;
handgeschriebener Brief; rotes Tuch über den
Tisch; Stuhl; 4 Kanäle „gespenstisches" Gemurmel
von 24 Lautsprecher gleichzeitig; Dunkelheit/com-
puter, monitor with running ghosts-dominated-screens-
aver program; telephone with an open receiver with non-
stop running audio message; slide projector, 80 slides,
constantly running in 1 sec. sequence; books about the
oeuvre of Bosch, Breugel, Dürer, Leonardo, Michelangelo,
Rubens and Jan van Eyck; press materials; magazines;
slides in plastic sleeves; T-shirt; cup of cold coffee; medi-
cine; ballpoint pens; Italian money; map of Berlin; desk
lamp; handwritten letter; red textile over table; chair;
4 channels 'ghostly' murmurings simultaneously played
from 24 loudspeakers; darkness; variable Dimensionen/
dimensions variable; Detail, Künstlerhaus Bethanien,
Berlin, 1995.
Courtesy der Künstler/the artist und/and Künstlerhaus Bethanien.

in afrika, there is a great man (black), collecting art from europe & america ...

The Collector of Art
1992; Aquarell, Tusche, Collage auf Papier/*watercolor, ink, collage on paper;* 21 x 29 cm. Collection Lubinus.

The Collector of Art (Somewhere in Africa there is a great black man collecting art from Europe and America, buying his Picasso for 23 coconuts and his early Rauschenberg for 7 antelope bones...)
1992-94; die Vorstellung einer afrikanischen Hütte, Sand, ausgetrocknete Büsche, Häute von giftigen Schlangen, Kokosnüsse, Ananas, Originale von Rauschenberg, Appel, Lichtenstein, Immendorff, Beuys, Baselitz, Picasso, Estes, Rainer, usw/*an idea of African hut, sand, dried up bushes, poisonous snakes' skins, coconuts, pineapples, original works by Rauschenberg, Appel, Lichtenstein, Immendorff, Beuys, Baselitz, Picasso, Estes, Rainer, etc; Detail, Ludwig Museum, Budapest, 1994.*
Courtesy der Künstler/*the artist* und/*and Ludwig Museum.*

The Collector of Art (Somewhere in Africa ...)
1992-2000; die Vorstellung einer afrikanischen Hütte, Sand, Zebrahaut, Kokosnüsse, Ananas, Kisten, Texte; Originale von Lichtenstein, Broodthaers, Kosuth, Flavin, Fabro, Filliou, Paolozzi, Viola, anonym – 16. Jahrhundert usw./*an idea of African hut, sand, zebra skin, coconuts, pineapples, crates, texts; original works by Lichtenstein, Broodthaers, Kosuth, Flavin, Fabro, Filliou, Paolozzi, Viola, anonym – 16th century, etc; „Partage d'exotismes," 5th Lyon Biennale, 2000.*
Collection Musee d'Art contemporain de Lyon.

THERE WAS NO electricity around, so he couldnt put on the D. FLAVIN's piece. But he still remembered the magic experience when he saw it for the first time. He PAY 27 white stones for it.

The M.B.'s WAS not so expensive – 12 giraffe skin's spots. (the giraffe, whose skin he used, died in a thunder storm)

Aus / From **New Noah's Ark**
1991-92 – „The Creatures", Thermoplastik/thermoplastic;
verschiedene Dimensionen/various dimensions;
Installation view – artist's studio, Sofia, 1992.

Solakov vor Solakov
Solakov before Solakov

The Crowd
1984; Öl auf Leinen/oil on linen;
73 x 92 cm. Sammlung Ludwig, Aachen.

Top Secret
1989-1990; Acrylfarbe, Tusche, Öl, Foto-
grafien, Graphit, Bronze, Aluminium,
Holz, ein schändliches Geheimnis; 176
Karteikarten im ursprünglichen Kasten/
acrylic, drawing ink, oil, photographs, graphite, bronze, aluminum, wood, shameful
secret; 176 slips mounted in original index box;
14 x 46 x 39 cm.
Courtesy der Künstler/the artist.

Der Zeitraum, den ich als „Solakov vor Solakov" be-
zeichne, erstreckt sich über ein Jahrzehnt, von Anfang
bis Ende der achtziger Jahre. Er beginnt 1981 mit dem
Studienabschluss des jungen bulgarischen Malers an der
Kunstakademie in Sofia, der bereits 1982 seine erste Einzelausstellung in der Galerie Rakowskistraße erhält, und
endet 1989, im Jahr des historischen Systemwechsels in
Bulgarien. In dieser Zeit entstehen zwei wichtige und
neuartige Arbeiten Solakovs, die seinen später einge-
schlagenen, konzeptuell geprägten Weg vorzeichnen: die
humorvoll-subversive Installation auf der Dachterasse
des Gebäudes des bulgarischen Künstlerverbandes „Blick
nach Westen" und der erst einige Monate nach der Wen-
de im Klub Junger Künstler ausgestellte und große Furore auslösende Objektkasten „Top Secret". Es sind diese
zehn Jahre, die in unserer Publikation nicht dokumentiert
sind, die jedoch eine entscheidende Periode in der künstlerischen Entwicklung Solakovs darstellen.

Ähnlich wie in den anderen osteuropäischen Ländern
hat sich auch die Situation der jungen Künstler in Bulgarien im Laufe der achtziger Jahre allmählich verändert.
Neben den obligatorischen Auftritten im Rahmen des
Künstlerverbandes und anderer staatlicher Institutionen
formierten sich die nichtoffiziellen Initiativen an alter-
nativen Orten. Solakov war von Anfang an einer der ak-
tivsten Teilnehmer an diesem Prozess und 1988 Gründ-
ungsmitglied der ersten freien Künstlervereinigung in
Sofia, „The City Group". Welch wichtige Rolle Solakov in-
nerhalb der Avantgardeszene Bulgariens in dieser Um-
bruchzeit gespielt und welche „entscheidende Impulse
für die Auseinandersetzung mit gegenwärtigen geistigen
und künstlerischen Strömungen" von seinem künstlerischen Schaffen ausging, beschrieb Barbara Barsch im Katalog zu seiner ersten Berliner Ausstellung 1992 in der
ifa-Galerie.

Meine erste Begegnung mit Nedko Solakovs Kunst war
1985 anlässlich der Ausstellung „Aspekte Bulgarischer
Kunst heute – Sammlung Ludwig", in welcher er mit
einem frühen Ölbild („Menschenmenge", 1982) vertreten
war. Schon damals stach Solakovs Bild mit seiner ironisch
kritischen Verfremdung des Themas aus der bunten Mischung von fadem Akademismus und Pseudomodernis-
mus heraus. Wir begegneten uns dann ein Jahr später

The period that I refer to as "Solakov before Solakov" extends
over the decade from the early to the late eighties. It begins in
1981, when the young Bulgarian painter graduated from his
studies at the Academy of Art in Sofia, already earning his
first one-man show in the gallery Rakovski Street in 1982,
and it ends in 1989, the year historical changes came about in
Bulgaria's political system. During this period Solakov produced
two important works of a new kind, works which mapped out
the conceptually characterised path he was to take later: the
humorously subversive installation on the roof terrace of the
building of the Bulgarian Artists' Association, "View to the
West", and the object case "Top Secret", which was shown a
few months after November 1989 at the Club of Young Artists
and which provoked considerable furore. These ten years, which
are not documented in our publication, nonetheless represent
a decisive period in Solakov's artistic development.

As was often the case in other eastern European countries as
well, the situation of young artists in Bulgaria gradually
changed in the course of the eighties. Alongside obligatory
appearances within the context of the Artists' Association and
other state institutions, non-official initiatives were formed
in alternative venues. From the beginning, Solakov was one of
the most active participants in this process. He was a found-
ing member of the first free artists' group in Sofia, "The City
Group". The important role Solakov played within the avantgarde scene in Bulgaria during this period of radical change,
and the "decisive impulses for an examination of contemporary intellectual and artistic tendencies" stimulated by his artistic work has been described by Barbara Barsch in the catalogue to his first Berlin exhibition at the ifa-galerie in 1992.

My first encounter with Nedko Solakov's art was in 1985, on
the occasion of the exhibition "Aspects of Bulgarian Art Today –
Ludwig Collection", where he was represented by an early oil
painting "The Crowd", 1982. At that time, Solakov's picture
with its ironic, critical alienation of the theme stood out among
the diverse mixture of dull academism and pseudo-modernism.
A year later, we met personally during my own visit to Sofia.
As a consequence of this meeting, I may now lay claim to the
privilege of having discovered Solakov for Germany; I organised
his first exhibition here as the director of the municipal gallery
in Esslingen during 1987.
Up until that time, his artistic activity was dominated by
the traditional techniques of painting and drawing (and there

persönlich bei meinem Besuch in Sofia. Als Folge dieses Treffens darf ich nun das Privileg in Anspruch nehmen, Solakov für Deutschland entdeckt zu haben, indem ich 1987 als Leiter der dortigen Städtischen Galerie seine erste Ausstellung in Esslingen organisierte.

Bis zu diesem Zeitpunkt dominierten die traditionellen Techniken, Malerei und Zeichnung (die er zweifelsohne meisterhaft beherrscht) seine künstlerische Tätigkeit. Er fand aber schon damals zu einem subversiven Stil (so reichte er z. B. das Bild einer Nacktschnecke zur Verbandsausstellung zum Thema „Akt") , der für seine Methode, vom eingesetzten Medium unabhängig, bis heute charakteristisch geblieben ist. Er verband das naive Folkloristische mit kommunistischer Ikonografie und ironisierte die damaligen visuellen Normen des „dekorativen" oder „monumentalen" Stils. Mit byzantinischer Lust am Ornament und am Fabulieren zeichnete er groteske Fabelwesen und absurde Situationen und kreierte so provokativ eine heitere Gegenwelt zu der trostlosen Wirklichkeit.

Ab 1988 begann in formaler Hinsicht eine neue Phase in Solakovs Werk. Er wandte sich anderen Techniken zu, beschäftigte sich mit Collagen, Objekten und Installationen, experimentierte mit den unterschiedlichsten Materialien und führte den geschriebenen Text in seine narrativen Arbeiten als zusätzliches Ausdruckmittel ein. Sein eingangs erwähntes Projekt „Blick nach Westen" war der Wendepunkt in seinem künstlerischen Reifungsprozess. Es verdeutlichte beispielhaft den folgerichtigen Zusammenhang von historischen Veränderungen in der Gesellschaft und dem Wirken des davon betroffenen Künstlers. Obwohl Solakov weiterhin der Malerei und Zeichnung treu blieb (wie auch diese Ausstellung belegt), entwickelte er im Laufe der folgenden Jahre eine eigenständige und facettenreiche Handschrift, die mit ihrer Mischung von Witz und Ernst, Klarheit und Komplexität, Präzision und Phantasie eine unverwechselbare Position in der Kunst der neunziger Jahre erobert hat. Und das ist letztendlich der „Solakov", den die Welt nach seiner ersten Vor-Solakov-Zeit kennengelernt hat.

Alexander Tolnay

is no doubt that he had mastered these extremely well). But at that time, he was already finding his way towards the subversive style (for example, he put forward a picture of a slug for the Association's exhibition with the theme "Nudes") which has remained characteristic of his method, quite independent of the medium employed, up until today. He combined the naïve folklorist with communist iconography and treated the visual norms of the "decorative" or "monumental" styles from that period in an ironical way. With a Byzantine desire for ornament and story-telling, he drew grotesque creatures of fable and absurd situations, thus provocatively creating a cheerful counter-world to the depressing reality.

With respect to form, a new phase of Solakov's work began in 1988. He turned to other techniques, investigating the effect of collages, objects and installations, experimenting with a wide variety of materials and introducing written text into his narrative works as additional expressive material. The project already mentioned, "View to the West", was the turning point in his artistic process towards maturity. In an exemplary way, it makes clear the consistent link between historical changes within society and the work of the artist effected by them. Although Solakov continued to remain faithful to painting and drawing (as this exhibition also demonstrates), in the course of the years that followed he developed an independent and many-faceted signature, which – with its mixture of wit and seriousness, clarity and complexity, precision and fantasy – has won an unmistakable position in the art of the nineties. And ultimately, this is the Solakov whom the world has come to know – after his first, "before Solakov" period.

Naked Body
1987; Öl und Graphit auf Leinen/oil and graphite on linen; 60 x 81 cm; Zerstört/Destroyed. Courtesy der Künstler/the artist.

View to the West
1989; Text, bronzene Tafel, ein Fernrohr, in Richtung Westen aufgestellt, der rote Stern oben auf dem Hauptgebäude der kommunistischen Partei Bulgariens, Sofia/ text, bronze plate, a telescope pointing west, the red star on the top of the Headquarters of the Bulgarian Communist Party, Sofia; Variable Dimensionen/dimensions variable; „The Earth and The Sky," The Club of Young Artists auf der Dachterrasse der Union of Bulgarian Artists' Shipka 6 Gallery. Teilweise zerstört/The Club of Young Artists on the roof terrace of the Union of Bulgarian Artists' Shipka 6 Gallery; Partly destroyed. Courtesy der Künstler/the artist.

Nedko Solakov

1957 born in Cherven Briag, Bulgaria · Studies at Academy of Fine Arts, Sofia **1981** Graduation in Mural Painting – Prof. Mito Ganovski **1985/1986** studies at Nationaal Hoger Instituut voor Schone Kunsten, Antwerp **1992** works in Zurich by a grant of Artest Foundation **1993** works in Austria by a grant of Kultur-Kontakt, Vienna **1994/1995** works in Künstlerhaus Bethanien, Berlin by a grant of Philip Morris Foundation **2001** works in Stockholm by a grant of IASPIS Lives and works in Sofia

Einzelausstellungen (Auswahl)/Selected One Person Exhibitions

2002 „Nature People," Museu do Chiado, Lisbon (C) · „Studies for Romantic Landscapes with Missing Parts," Galerie Arndt & Partner, Berlin · „Romantic Landscapes with Missing Parts," Neuer Berliner Kunstverein, Berlin; Ulmer Museum, Ulm (C) · „20.10.2001," Galerie Erna Hecey, Luxembourg **2001** „Chat," The Royal Academy Sculpture Hall/IASPIS Gallery, Stockholm (C) · „Vitiligo People," Galleria Laura Pecci, Milano · „Marginalia," Modulo Centro Difusor de Arte, Lisbon · „A (not so) White Cube," P.S.1 Special Projects Program, P.S.1 Contemporary Art Center, New York · „Anywhere," Tanya Rumpff Gallery, Haarlem, NL **2000** „Stories 1," Center for Contemporary Art, Ujazdowski Castle, Warsaw (C) · „Squared Baroque – Baroqued Square," Ikonen-Museum/Portikus, Frankfurt am Main (C) · „El Bulgaro," Galerie Arndt & Partner, Project Rooms/ARCO, Madrid (C) **1999** „......." #2, Galerija Dante Marino Cettina, Umag, Croatia · „Announcement," as the official participation of Bulgaria, La Biennale di Venezia, Venice (C) · „......," ATA Center for Contemporary Art, Sofia (C) **1998** „A Christmas Show," Galerie arsFutura, Zurich · „Silly," Galerie Arndt & Partner, Berlin · „Sea Show," Ted Gallery, Varna (with Slava Nakovska) · „A Quiz," De Vleeshal, Middelburg, NL · „Thirteen (maybe)," Musee Nationale d'Historie et d'Art, Luxembourg (C) **1997** „Yellow," Galerija Anonimus, Ljubljana · „The Paranoid Man," Galerie Georges-Philippe & Nathalie Vallois, Paris · „The Absent-Minded Man," FRAC Languedoc-Roussillon, Montpellier · „Wars," Galerie Erna Hecey, Luxembourg · „Somewhere (under the tree)," Deitch Projects, New York · „By the way," Art Connexion, Lille (C) **1996** „Semipoor-Semirich," The Swiss Ambassador's residence, Sofia · „Desires," Galerie Arndt & Partner, Berlin (C) · „Doodles," National Museum of Fine Arts' mirrors, Sofia **1995** „To Touch the Antiquity," Ata-Ray Gallery, Sofia · „Mr. Curator, please....," Studio I, Künstlerhaus Bethanien, Berlin (C) **1994** „The Superstitious Man," Center for Curatorial Studies, Bard College, Annandale-on-Hudson, NY · „Documentation," Ata-Ray Gallery, Sofia · „The Collector of Art," Ludwig Museum, Budapest (C) · „The Superstitious Man," Museum of Contemporary Art, Skopje (C) · „Notes," National Palace of Culture's toilets, Sofia · „Bulgarian-American Souvenirs," American Center, Sofia **1993** „Their Mythological Highnesses," Ata-Ray Gallery, Sofia · „Les aventures (et les visions) de Francois de La Bergeron en terre Bulgare," French Institute, Sofia · „4 (maybe 5) Room Installations," Elemag 2D Gallery, Sofia · Lessedra Gallery, Sofia (with Mitjo Solakov) · „Good Luck," Medizinhistorisches Museum, Zurich **1992** „Just Imagine," BINZ 39/Artest, Zurich · „Neue Arche Noah," ifa Galerie, Berlin (C) · „Nine Objects," National Museum of History, Sofia · „7 Paintings, 13 Reliquaries, 1 Installation (New Noah's Ark)," National Palace of Culture, Sofia **1990** „Objects," AIA Gallery, Bourgas, BG **1988** „Autumn Exhibitions," Plovdiv, BG (C) · Shipka 6 Gallery, Sofia **1987** Bahnwärterhaus, Esslingen am Neckar **1985** The City Square Gallery, Varna, BG **1983** „Autumn Exhibitions," Plovdiv, BG **1982** Rakovski 108 Gallery, Sofia

Ausstellungsbeteiligungen (Auswahl)/Selected Group Exhibitions

2002 „Power," Casino Luxembourg – Forum d'art Contemporain, Luxembourg (curators D. L. Harten, E. Lunghi) (C) · Museum für Moderne Kunst, Frankfurt am Main (curator U. Kittelmann) (C) · „Loop," Contemporary Art Center, Cincinnati, Ohio (curator K. Biesenbach) (C) · „Reconstructions," 4th Cetinje Biennial, Cetinje (curators I. Boubnova, A. Erofeev) (C) · „Frenetic Interferences – Memory/Cage Editions," New Museum of Contemporary Art, New York (curators D. Kurjakovic, A. Notz) · „Pause," 4th Gwangju Biennale, Gwangju (curators W. Sung, C. Esche, H. Hanru) (C) · „Basics," Kunsthalle Bern, Bern (curator B. Fibicher) (C) · „Socle du Monde," Herning Art Museum, Herning, Denmark (curator H. Reenberg) (C) **2001** „Marking the Territory," Irish Museum of Modern Art, Dublin (curator M. Abramovic) (C) · „Loop – Alles auf Anfang," Kunsthalle der Hypo-Kulturstiftung, Munich; P.S. 1, New York (curator K. Biesenbach) (C) · „Total Object Complete with Missing Parts," Tramway, Glasgow (curator A. Renton) (C) · „A World within a Space," Kunsthalle Zurich, Zurich (curator D.l Kurjakovic) (C) · „Wir sind die Ander(en)," various sites, Herford (curator J. Hoet) (C) · „Devoler," Institute of Contemporary Art in Villeurbanne, Lyon (curator A. Barak) · „Empathy – Beyond the Horizon," Pori Art Museum, Pori, Finland (curator M. Seppala) (C) · „Plateau of Humankind," 49 Esposizione Internazionale d'Arte, La Biennale di Venezia, Venice (curator H. Szeemann) (C) · „Locus/Focus," Sonsbeek 9, Arnhem, NL (curator J. Hoet) (C) · „Every Day There Is Something Different," Galerie Erna Hecey, Luxembourg **2000** „Bricolage?," FRAC Bourgogne/Musee des Beaux-Arts, Dijon (curator E. Latreille) (C) · „The Last Drawing of the Century (A Window onto Venus)," Zerynthia, 6th Biennale of Havana (C) · „Leaving the Island," Pusan Metropolitan Art Museum, Pusan, Korea (curators R. Martinez, H. Hanru, Y. C. Lee) (C) · „Waterfront/Cultural Bridge 2000," various sites, Helsingborg/Helsingor, Sweden/Denmark (curator P. Kyander) (C) · „Amorales, Melgaard, Rawanchaikul, Solakov, Ozawa, Xhafa," Galleria Laura Pecci, Milano · „Premio Michetti 2000," Fondazione Michetti, Francavilla al Mare, Chieti, Italy (curator Gianni Romano) (C) · „Storm Centers – Poeziezomers Watou," Watou, Belgium (curator J. Hoet) (C) · „Partage d'exotismes," 5e Biennale de Lyon, Lyon (curator J.-H. Martin) (C) · „Arteast 2000+/The New Collection," Moderna Galerija, Ljubljana (curator Z. Badovinac) (C) · „3 Räume – 3 Flüsse," various sites, Hann. Münden, Germany (curator J. Hoet) (C) · „Drawing on the Figure: Works on Paper of the 1990s from the Manilow Collection," MCA Chicago (curator S. Boris) (C) · „L'Autre moitie de l'Europe," Jeu de Paume, Paris (curators Lorand Hegyi, Viktor Misiano, Anda Rottenberg) (CD-ROM catalogue) · „Video Positive 2000: The Other Side of Zero," FACT, Liverpool (curators committee) (C) **1999** „Jahresgaben", Frankfurter Kunstverein, Frankfurt am Main (curator N. Schafhausen) (C) · „Zeitwenden – Looking forward into the next millennium," Kunstmuseum Bonn, Bonn; (curators committee) (C) · „Locally Interested," ICA/National Gallery for Foreign Art, Sofia (curator I. Boubnova) (C) · „After the Wall," Moderna Museet, Stockholm; Ludwig Museum, Budapest; Hamburger Bahnhof, Berlin (curators B. Pejic, D. Elliott) (C) · „Turning the Page," Apollonia Festival of Arts, Sozopol (curator D. Dimova) (C) · „Faiseurs d'histoires," Casino Luxembourg – Forum d'art Contemporain, Luxembourg (curators committee) (C) · „Fauna," The Zacheta Gallery of Contemporary Art, Warsaw (curators Mindlin, Rottenberg, Kardasz) (C) · „Recipes," Institute of Contemporary Art, Sofia (curator M. Vassileva) · „Rondo," Ludwig Museum/Museum of Contemporary Art, Budapest (curators K. Neray & team) (C) · „Un certain art de vivre" (from the collection of FRAC Languedoc-Roussillon), Ata Center for Arts, Ata-Ray, Sofia (traveled) (C) **1998** „MoneyNations@access," Shedhalle, Zurich (curator M. v. Osten) (C) · „Magic Carpet," Malmö Konstmuseet, Malmö (curators C. Esche & team) (C) · 7. Triennale der Kleinplastik, Zudwest LB, Stuttgart (curator W. Meyer) (C) · „Revolution – Terror," ISEA'98, Liverpool/Manchester, Castlefield Gallery, Manchester (curator C. Esche) (C) · „Medialization," Edsvik Konst. Kultur, Sollentuna, Stockholm; Eesti Kunstimuuseum, Tallinn (curator J. Backstein) (C) · „Kräftemessen 2: Bulgariaavantgarde," Künstlerwerkstatt Lothringerstrasse, Munich (curator I. Boubnova) (C) · „A Century of Artistic Freedom," Wiener Secession, Vienna; Helsinki City Art Museum, Helsinki (curator R. Fleck) (C) **1999** „a vendre;" Galerie Erna Hecey, Luxembourg · „Heaven – Private View," P.S.1 Contemporary Art Center, New York (curator J. Decter) · „Unmapping the Earth," Kwangju Biennale'97, Kwangju (curator S. W. Kyung) (C) · „Splash! - N. Solakov, P. Sorin, G. Wearing," ACC Galerie, Weimar (curators F. Motz, A. Dietrich, M.-R. Hopkins) (CD-ROM catalogue) · „Ars Ex Natio," SCA, The Old City of Plovdiv (curators I. Boubnova, M. Vassileva) (C) · „Around Us, Inside Us," Boras Konstmuseum, Boras (curators E. Haglund, C. Capelan) (C) · „S/light," Malmö Konstmuseet, Malmö (curator P. Herbstreuth) (C) **1996** „Enclosures," The New Museum of Contemporary Art, New York (curator D. Cameron) (C) · „The Scream/Borealis 8," Arken Museum of Modern Art, Copenhagen (curator K. Levin) (C) · „Inklusion : Exklusion," Künstlerhaus Graz, Steirischer Herbst'96, Graz (curator P. Weibel) (C) · „Instant Replay," Galerie Arndt & Partner, Berlin · „Manifesta I," Natuur Museum, Rotterdam (curators R. Martinez, V. Misiano, K. Neray, H. U. Obrist, A. Renton) (C) · „The Sense of Order," Moderna Galerija, Ljubljana (curator Z. Badovinac) (C) · „Beyond Belief," Allen Memorial Art Museum, Oberlin College; ICA, Philadelphia (curator L. J. Hoptman) (C) **1995** „Orient/ation," 4th Istanbul Biennial (curators R. Block, I. Boubnova) (C) · „The Image of Europe," Nicosia streets, Cyprus (curator G. Romano) (C) · „Beyond Belief," Museum of Contemporary Art, Chicago (curators L. J. Hoptman, R. Francis) (C) · „Caravanseray of Contemporary Art," Fuori Uso/Aurum, Pescara (curator G. D. Pietrantonio) (C) · „Club Berlin – Kunst Werke," 46 Esposizione Internazionale d'Arte, La Biennale di Venezia, Venice (curator K. Biesenbach) · „Projects," National Gallery for Foreign Art,

Sofia (curator I. Boubnova) · „The Outburst of Signs," Künstlerwerkstatt Lothringerstrasse, Munich (curators M. Fauss, P. Lanzinger, A. Loebell) (C) **1994** „N Forms? Reconstructions and Interpretations," SCA/Raiko Alexiev Gallery, Sofia (C) · „22 Bienal," Sao Paulo (curators Nelson A., I. Boubnova) (C) · „Europa'94," MOC, Munich (curators C. Gögger, B. Gross, K. Pfefferle, W. Storms, B. Wittenbrink) (C) · „In Search of Self-Reflection," Plovdiv (curator I. Boubnova) · „Naturally," Ernst Museum, Budapest (curators K. Keseru, M. Papp) (C) · „Dermatology ? Art," Medical Faculty – Department of Dermatology, Sofia (curator Dr. Med. G. Gatev) (C) **1993** „Object – Bulgarian Way," Club of the (Eternally) Young Artists, Sofia (curators I. Boubnova, D. Popova, M. Vassileva) · „Works on Paper," Ata-Ray Gallery, Sofia (curator I. Boubnova) · „Übergänge," Museum Moderner Kunst, Passau (curators H. Knoll, I. Boubnova) · „Exchange II," Shedhalle, Zurich (curator H. Lux) · „Aperto'93," La Biennale di Venezia, Venice (curators H. Kontova, K. Changan) (C) · „Schaerf, Wüthrich, Solakov, Widoff, Tison," Shedhalle, Zurich (curator H. Lux) (C) **1992** 3rd Istanbul Biennial (curators V. Kortun, L. Boyadjiev) (C) · „Hair from a Brush," Club of the (Eternally) Young Artists, Shipka 6 Gallery, Sofia (curator L. Boyadjiev) · „From a Moment of Truth…," Karl Drerup Gallery, Plimouth State College, Plimouth, USA (curator R. Weiss) **1991** „Kaimak (Top) Art," Shipka 6 Gallery, Sofia · „Summer Exhibitions of the City Group," various venues, Sofia · „Europe Unknown," Palac Sztuki, Cracow (curators A. Rottenberg, L. Boyadjiev, P. Zidarov) (C) **1990** „Expressions," Third Eye Centre, Glasgow (curator A. Nairne) (C) · „Top Secret," Action with Colleagues, Sofia · „The End of the Quotation," Club of the (Eternally) Young Artists, Sofia (curator L. Boyadjiev) · „10 x 10 x 10," Club of the (Eternally) Young Artists, Sofia (curator Georgi) · „First Exposition of The City Group," The City Gallery, Rakovski 134, Sofia · „The Chameleon," Action with The City Group, Sofia **1989** „11. 11," Municipal Art Gallery, Blagoevgrad, BG · „The Earth and The Sky," Shipka 6 Gallery, Sofia (curators Georgi, D. Popova) · „The Tower of Babylon," Action with The City Group, Gabrovo, BG **1988** „The City ?," Rakovski 125 Gallery, Sofia (curator P. Zidarov) **1985** „Young Bulgarian Artists," Witgensteinhaus, Vienna **1984** „Aspekte Bulgarischer Kunst Heute – Sammlung Ludwig," Künstlerhaus Wien; Villa Merkel, Esslingen (C)   (C)   *a catalog published*

Werke in öffentlichen Sammlungen/Selected Public Collections

Center for Contemporary Art, Ujazdowski Castle, Warsaw · De Vleeshal, Middelburg, NL · Fonds National d'Art Contemporain, Paris · FRAC Bourgogne, Dijon · FRAC Languedoc-Roussillon, Montpellier · Joslyn Art Museum, Omaha, USA · Ludwig Museum, Aachen · Ludwig Museum, Budapest · Moderna Galerija, Ljubljana · Musee d'Art contemporain de Lyon · Museum für Moderne Kunst, Frankfurt am Main · Museum moderner Kunst Stiftung Ludwig Wien · National Gallery of Fine Arts, Sofia · Natuur Museum, Rotterdam · Sammlung Hauser und Wirth, St. Gallen · Teyler Museum, Haarlem, NL · The City Art Gallery, Sofia · The Museum of Contemporary Art, Skopje · The Museum of Fine Arts, Budapest · The Museum of Modern Art, Department of Prints and Illustrated Books, New York · The National Library, Luxembourg · The New Museum of Contemporary Art, New York · Villa Merkel, Esslingen am Neckar, Germany

Bibliogaphie (Auswahl)/Selected Bibliography

Solakov, Nedko. Night Notes with a Pain in the Back. New Observations, September-October 1992 · Levin, Kim. Significant Others in Istanbul. Village voice, 1.12.1992 · Anderson, Geneva. New Noah' s Ark. ARTnews, January 1993 · Dannatt, Adriann. Turkish Biennial. Flash Art, 168, January/February 1993 · Kravagna, Christian. 3- rd Istanbul Biennale. Kunstforum, 121, 1993 · McFadden, Sarah. Bosporus Dialogues. Art in America, June 1993 · Danailov, Boris. Nedko Solakov. Flash Art, Summer 1993 · Anderson, Geneva. Dossier – Sofia. Sculpture, July 1993 · McEvilley, Thomas. Arrivederci Venice. Art Forum, November, 1993 · Metzger, Rainer. Europa'94. Kunstforum International, 128, October/December 1994 · Solakov, Nedko. La Verdad, La Terra es Plana, el Mundo es Liso. Accion Paralela, 1, 1995 · Tannert, Christoph. Nedko Solakov: „Mr. Curator, please…." Neue Bildende Kunst, 3, 1995 · Herbstreuth, Peter. Nedko Solakov. Kunstforum International, 131, 1995 · Levin, Kim. Nedko Solakov – Honest Fictions. BE Magazine, 3, 1995 · Fricke, Harald. Nedko Solakov. Artforum, December 1995 · Murphy, Jay. Beyond Belief. World Art, 1, 1996 · Heartney, Eleanor. Istanbul – 4th Biennial. Art Press, February 1996 · Volk, Gregory. Istanbul Biennial… Art in America, May 1996 · Grauman, Brigid. A Collective „Manifesta" on Art. The Wall Street Journal, 5.7.1996 · Pirman, Alenka. „The Sense of Order". Sculpture, October 1996 · Morgan, Stuart. Manifesta. frieze, October 1996 · Cameron, Dan, Gerardo Mosquera. Enclosures. The New Museum of Contemporary Art, New York, November 1996 · Potrc, Marjetica. Everybody Would Like to Have Some Kind of Fairy Tales. MARS, Moderna Galerija Ljubljana, 3/4, 1996 · Enwezor, Okwui. Inclusion/Exclusion …. frieze, 33, March/April 1997 · Smith, Robertha. Despite Changes, a Gallery Scene That's Resilient and Vital. The New York Times, 9.5.1997 · Levin, Kim. Art Short List. The Village Voice, 20.5.1997 · Solakov, Nedko. The Thief of Art. Zingmagazine, Summer 1997 · Phillips, Christopher. Report from Sofia – The View from Europe's Lower East Side. Art n America, October 1997 · Millet, Cathrine. Unmapping the Earth – biennale de Kwangju. Art Press, December 1997 · Cameron, Dan. Glocal Warming. Art Forum, December 1997 · Nottrot, Ina. Kriegsgeschichten – Neue Arbeiten von Nedko Solakow. Neue Bildende Kunst, 6, 1997 · Hoffman, Justin. Bulgariaavantgarde. Kunstforum, 141, 1998 · Dannatt, Adrian. Nedko Solakov. Flash Art – Global Art, Summer 1998 · McClellan, Jim. It's about art, not gizmos. The Gardian, 27.8.1998 · Solakov, Nedko. Letter from Sofia. Flash Art/News, October 1998 · Ebeling, Knut. Nach dem Fall der Götter. Der Tagesspiegel, Berlin, 31.10.1998 · Zeit – Reise in die Zukunft. Die Zeit, Hamburg, 30.12.1998 · Romano, Gianni. Bloom: Contemporary Art Garden. Gotham – Milano, February 1999 · Solakov, Nedko. Some Stories. Vlasblom & Partners, Netherlands, June 1999 · Levin, Kim. Rebirth in Venice. The Village Voice, 23-29.6.1999 · Millet, Catherine. La Biennale – 48e exposition internationale d'art. Art Press, September 1999 · Birnbaum, Daniel. Preview – After the Wall. Artforum, September, 1999 · Faiseurs d'histoires im Casino. Kunst-Bulletin, October 1999 · Heartney, Eleanor. Berlin: Future Perfect? Art in America, February 2000 · Dimova, Dessislava. Locally Interested. Flash Art, March/April 2000 · Brown, N., Il. Nedkova, Dr. Al. Bleakley, Ch. Esche. Essays on Solakov's The Right One CD-ROM. AVRE/FACT, Liverpool, March 2000 · Snodgrass, Susan. Post-Communist Expressions. Art in America, June 2000 · Vetrocq, Marcia E. East is East. Art in America, June 2000 · Cruewell, Konstanze. Drei Heilige mit der Sehnsucht nach Einsamkeit. Frankfurter Allgemeine Zeitung, 24.6.2000 · Breerette, Genevieve. La Cinquieme Biennale de Lyon, exotique avec humour. Le Monde, 30.6.2000 · Riding, Alan. „Exotic"? Perhaps, Yet Neither Primitive Nor Pure. The New York Times, 5.7.2000 · Sotriffer, Kristian. Wie Kunst in das neue Saekulum ausgrast. Die Presse, Vienna, 6.7.2000 · Riding, Alan. New Definition of Exoticism. International Herald Tribune, 8–9. 7. 2000 · Herzog, Samuel. Biennale von Lyon. Babylonische Suppe. Der Tagesspiegel, 13.7.2000 · Genies, Bernard. Le tour de monde de la creation. Le Nouvel Observateur, 20-26.7.2000 · Herzog, Samuel. Frische babylonische Buchstabensuppe. Neue Zuercher Zeitung, 22-23.7.2000 · Levin, Kim. Border Crossings. Village Voice, 1.8.2000 · Martinez, Rosa. Who Doesn't Like Stories? On Nedko Solakov. ARCO Noticias, 18, September 2000 · Heartney, Eleanor. An Adieu to Cultural Purity. Art in America, October 2000 · Noe, Paola. The 5th Lyons Biennial. Tema Celeste, October/December 2000 · Robecchi, Michele. The Fifth Lyon Biennial. Flash Art/News, 215, November/December 2000 · Siemons, Mark. Still a Separate Continent. Frankfurter Allgemeine Zeitung, 5.11.2000 · FRESH CREAM – Contemporary Art in Culture. Phaidon Press, London, 2000 · Volk, Gregory. Nedko Solakov. Art in America, December 2000 · Thea, Carolee. 5th Lyon Biennale. Sculpture, December 2000 · Wolodzko, Agnieszka. Nedko Solakov at Ujazdowski Castle. Flash Art/News, March 2001 · Gibbs, Michael. Collected Jokes – on Nedko Solakov's new CD ROM „The Right One".Art Monthly, April, 2001 · Schulze, Karin. Schlangen, Seelenhaeuser und Sisyphus. Financial Times Deutschland, 12.6.2001 · Nuridsany, Michel. Coup de jeune pour la biennale! Le Figaro, 15.6.2001 · 49th Venice Biennale. Euronews Cult, 16./17.6.2001 · Hughes Meyric, Henry. Venice Biennale – A Concert of Variety. Tema Celeste, Summer, 2001 · Biennale Venedig – Plateau der Menschheit. Frame, August/September, 2001 · Wulffen, Thomas. Biennale Venedig: Plateau der Menschheit. Kunstforum International, 156, August/October, 2001 · Millet, Catherine. 49e biennale de Venise. Art Press, September 2001 · Mahoney, Elizabeth. Total Object Complete with Missing Parts. The Guardian, 13.9.2001 · Meier, Philipp. Einübung ins Zur-Welt-Kommen: Raumwelten in der Kunsthalle. Neue Zürcher Zeitung, 24.9.2001 · Mahoney, Elizabeth. Total Object Complete with Missing Parts. Art Monthly, 250, October 2001 · Nilsson, John Peter. The 49th Venice Biennial x 2. nu: The Nordic Art Review, 5, 2001 · Scardi, Gabi. Biennale/Solakov – Diatribe tra il bianco e il nero. Il Solle – 24 ore, Milano, 14.10.2001 · Dunne, Aidan. Marking the Territory. The Irish Times, 17.10.2001 · Müller, Silke. Loop – Alles auf Anfang. Gefangen in der Schleife. Art, 11, November 2001 · Cherubini, Laura. Nedko Solakov. Tema Celeste, November/December 2001 · Scardi, Gabi. Nedko Solakov. Flash Art/Italian Edition, December 2001/January 2002 · Hofner, Hans-Jürgen. Loop – Alles auf Anfang. Kunstforum International, 158, January/February 2002 · Sonna, Birgit. Endlos Rotierende Tranquilizer – Loop Alles auf Anfang. Frame, January/March 2002

Aus/From **Marginalia**
2001; Einzelausstellung/one-person exhibition;
Modulo Centro Difusor de Arte, Lisbon.